INGRES User Guide
Visual Programming Tools

INGRES User Guide
Visual Programming Tools

Peter Matthews
UNIX systems group manager for
INGRES International Operations
European Technical Centre

Prentice Hall
New York   London   Toronto   Sydney   Tokyo   Singapore

First published 1991 by
Prentice Hall International (UK) Ltd
66 Wood Lane End, Hemel Hempstead
Hertfordshire HP2 4RG

A division of
Simon & Schuster International Group

NOTICE
The author and the publisher have used their best efforts to prepare
the book, including the computer examples contained in it. The
computer examples have been tested. The author and the publisher
make no warranty, implicit or explicit, about the documentation.
The author and the publisher will not be liable under any
circumstances for any direct or indirect damages arising from any
use, direct or indirect of the documentation or the computer
examples contained in this book.

INGRES is a trademark of INGRES Corporation Inc.

UNIX is a registered trademark of AT&T Bell Laboratories
in the USA and other countries.

Computer hardware and software brand names and company
names mentioned in this book are protected by their respective
trademarks and are acknowledged.

Printed and bound in Great Britain by Page Bros, Norwich

Library of Congress Cataloging-in-Publication Data

Mathews, Peter.
    INGRES user guide : visual programming tools / Peter Mathews.
      p. cm.
    Includes bibliographical references and index.
    ISBN 0–13–463720–8
    1. Data base management.   2. INGRES (Computer system)
    3. Relational data bases.   I. Title.
    QA76.9.D3M386   1991
    005.75'65—dc20   90–7407
                                               CIP

British Library Cataloguing in Publication Data

Mathews, Peter
    INGRES user guide : visual programming tools
    1. Databases. Management
    I. Title
    005.74

ISBN 0–13–463720–8

---

1 2 3 4 5 94 93 92 91

For my wife Pat

Acknowledgements

This book owes much to Mike Cash at Prentice Hall for his patience, and especially to my collegues and friends at Ingres for their help and assistance, freely given. Special thanks must go to Carlos Miguens, Martin Wallis and Mansel Jones at Ingres for their comments and advice.

Contents

Chapter 1

Introduction

1.1 Introduction

1.1.1 About this book

Conceived in principle a long time ago, this book was developed from a simple idea: how useful it would be if there were a simple book to tell people how to use this complex product, INGRES.

This is a simple book. Each of the chapters explains the use of INGRES menu driven systems building on information in the previous chapter. This allows the reader to build up a complex application quickly and easily. As part of the step-by-step approach the user is taken painlessly through designing and building a database, populating it with tables, and filling the tables with data. After the reader has created screen forms and reports for data input and output, there is a short section on linking all these together to make a complete application. This is not intended as a basic text about databases, relational algebra, or even a high brow discussion on query optimization. There will be some need to cover these points, but only where they will aid the understanding of terms used in the book. This book is a simple user text, and and is intended to be **used**.

1.1.2 Who should read this book?

Anyone reading this book should have some basic computer literacy, but not necessarily in depth. As this is a user text, the person reading it should simply be a user. If you already know all about INGRES, then you probably already know more than the book covers.

If you have a practical requirement for these skills, so much the better, for you can apply your skills to real problems while you are reading. Anyone with access to INGRES can use this book to develop their own applications, which may be trivial to programmers, but fulfil a real need.

This book is aimed at the people who are new to INGRES. People who may want to "play" for a while, developing their own applications. Their reasons are likely to be many. In fact anyone who has an interest in INGRES would benefit from working through this book.

1.1.3 How to read this book

The key words introduced in the previous section are **simple** and **working**. This book is constructed around a series of step-by-step exercises designed to clarify and reinforce skills developed in the chapters. It is possible to read each chapter in isolation and follow the exercises, but most of the exercises follow in sequence and are easier to work with in that sequence. If you already have relational database design experience, or are only reading this book to find out a little about INGRES, you can skip the chapter on Database Design. Appendix A has database design details that can be used in all the other exercises.

It is also a **users'** book. The point of this users' book is to help you get practical experience in developing an application, using INGRES Forms and Menu based tools to build an application.

You will start by designing and building a database structure. Next you will learn how to get data into and out of that database, followed by some cosmetic surgery on screens for data manipulation. Then you learn how to produce reports and tie all the reports and screens together in an application with a menu to drive it. So there it is. Now you know what you have paid for: a users' guide to the INGRES front end tools. The term **front end** has been used frequently up until now without definition.

A front end in this context is a user interface to the INGRES database management system.

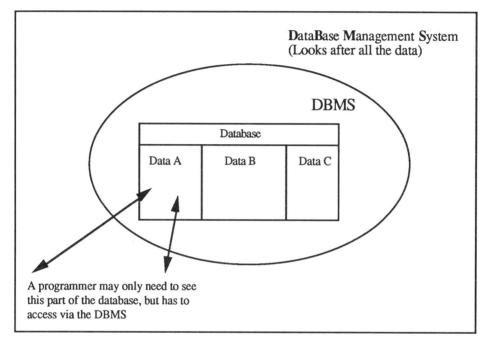

Figure 1.1 Database management system

1.2 What is a Database Management System?

1.2.1 Databases

Over the years the term databank or database has come to mean a group of data held by an organization. A database can be used to refer to all the data in a corporate system, or only a department's sales data. Each database is made up of a series of data items held in an organized way. This facilitates retrieval of existing data or the addition of new data.

1.2.2 Data items

A data item is the smallest unit of data in the database. There is an additional qualification that this small unit of data must have meaning to the user. It is no good having a database that records all the sales details for your company and a data item that represents the amount of pasta

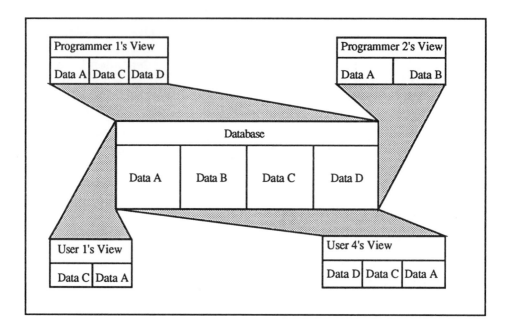

Figure 1.2 Application independence

consumed in the company restaurant. Every company or organization has a database and relevant data items, but not every company has a computer based database.

1.2.3 Database management systems

A computer based database can be built at vast expense by the use of clever application programs and the use of large data processing departments. Nostalgics can probably hear the click of a thousand card punches. However things have moved on a little from there. We now understand that knowledge is power, so the more accessible knowledge is, the better for the power hungry. To make this knowledge accessible we need a method of maintaining information independently of the application programmer. This is the database management system. The database management system (DBMS) acts as an interface between the application program, and maintains the data independently of the programs that access it. Figure 1.1 illustrates the concept more fully. This gives a number of advantages, but the chief ones are **data independence** and **central administration**.

Data independence is a term applied to data that is not dependent on one special program for its maintenance. For example in a payroll system the data is dependent on the payroll program that maintains it, whereas in a payroll database that data can be updated, deleted and extracted independently of the payroll program. This illustrates **data independence**.

Central administration of data gives the ability to backup, copy and manipulate data from a central point, without all the special programs that manipulate individual data items. As you can see from Figure 1.2 each programmer's view of the data is different. This system would require four separate programs to manage the data if access were not through a DBMS (DataBase Management System) and probably another program to maintain the data integrity.

1.3 What is a Relational Database?

This question can best be answered by a quick step into history. In 1485 King Richard III of England lost his head and most of the rest of him on Bosworth Field. However this has little to do with databases, unless you work for a museum or travel agency. The kind of history I am talking about is fairly recent, going back only to 6th June 1970, when a bombshell landed on the awestruck world. Yes, Ted Codd's paper "A

Relational Model of Data for Large Shared Data Banks" hit the streets. Now, who will confess to not having a copy only hours after publication? Me for one, and most of the people who were still at school, too. However in simple terms that is when it all started.

1.3.1 The Coddfather?

In a number of papers between 1970 and 1972 Codd developed the initial ideas behind the relational database concepts. One of the most useful parts of Codd's work was to describe the technique of normalization. Normailzation is a technique for simplifying complex data structures into a number of two-dimensional tables of data. This technique produces a clear, easy to understand, **logical** view of data. A **logical** view of the data already implies data independence, as you can see in Figure 1.2. It is important at this time to understand that a logical description of the data is different from the physical description of the data. The database management system takes care of the physical description of the data, which part of which disk and file the item is held in. Normalization helps to develop the logical description of data, based on relating similar types of data. A **relational** database management system links the logical, relational view with the physical view of the data.

1.3.2 Relations

The term relation is applied to the tabular representation of data that is used to describe logical data. Representing data in tabular form is often the most natural way. We are all familiar with train timetables and tax tables.

A table of data is called a **relation**, as all the data are related in a two-dimensional form, as in Figure 1.3. If the data cannot be represented in a two-dimensional table, the techique of normalization will enable you to split the table into two or more tables. Don't worry about losing data, as we will be discussing joining logical tables together to solve this problem. In this book we will use the term **table**, rather than **relation**, as it is more easily understood. A table can be equated to a flat file in data processing terms. A flat file is a data processing file that has no index, and all the records are of the same type.

1.3.3 Columns

Each table is made up of a number of columns. Each column represents a distinct different type of data and is unique for that table. A column is called a domain in relational algebra. It can be equated to a field in a flat file. Normally one of the columns in a table contains the unique identifier to each row. The column that holds this identifier is called the primary key.

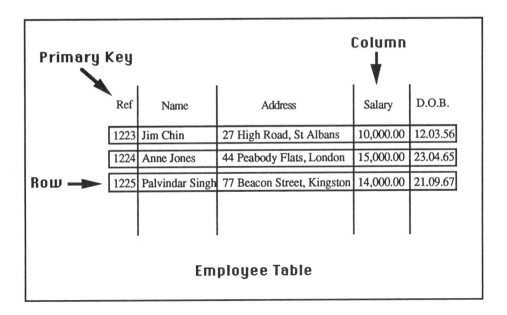

Figure 1.3 A table of data showing rows and columns

1.3.4 Rows

Each table is made up of a number of rows. Each row in a table must be unique, therefore its position in the table doesn't matter, as the row can always be retrieved by its unique identifier. This identifier is called the key. The correct relational term for a row is a tuple. We will use the term row in this book, but remember the term tuple if you are going deeper into the jungle that is relational algebra. In ordinary terms a row can be equated with a record in an unstructured file.

1.3.5 Projections

If you look at Figure 1.4 you can see that, although it shows a row from the employee table in Figure 1.3, it could be viewed as two tables. Each of these views of the data contains a subset of the data from the employee table. The views are not normally physical tables, as that would be a waste of space, but a logical view of data. This production of new logical tables from one base table is called **projection**. This is the way that mailing labels are prepared from personnel files, without all the interesting stuff about salary and age appearing on an envelope.

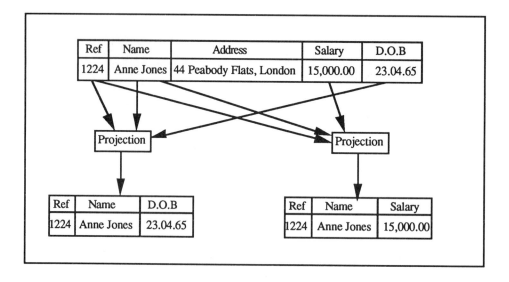

Figure 1.4 Projection of data from a single table

1.3.6 Joins

A **projection** is one way of producing a new view of data. The other method, which will produce a new view of data from two or more tables, is called a **join**. A **join** can be thought of as a link between tables based on a common value. If the value of one column in a row matches the value in a column of a row of the other tables then the data from both tables can be combined as a new logical row. If this seems a little

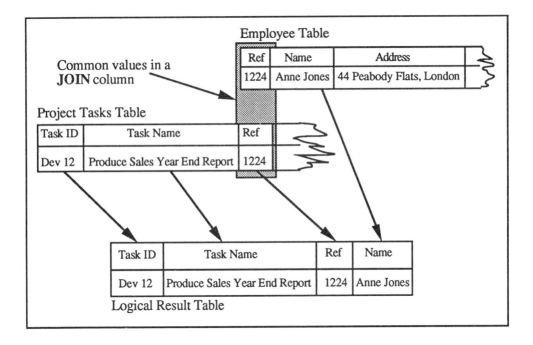

Figure 1.5 Two tables joined

complicated, have a look at Figure 1.5, which shows how two tables are logically **joined** together. Again the result table is logical not physical.

An important point to remember about joins is that joins will not give any result if there are no matching values in the join columns of the rows. In this case there is no join.

It is possible to join more than two tables together, as long as there are common values in the columns. Figure 1.6 shows a three table join, and the principle of joining more than three tables together is the same. Some RDBMS (**R**elational **D**ata**B**ase **M**anagement **S**ystems) place restrictions on the number of tables that you can join together, but this is a physical limitation.

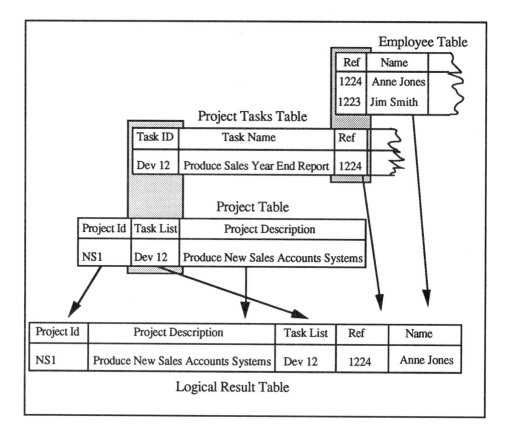

Figure 1.6 Three tables joined

There is no logical limitation to the number of tables you can join together. You can even join a table to itself.

1.4 What is INGRES?

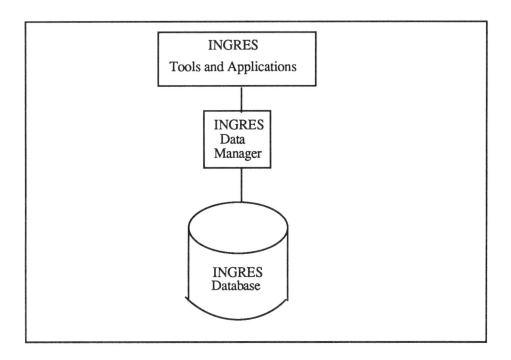

Figure 1.7 Basic structure of INGRES

1.4.1. A relational database management system

INGRES is a relational database management system which combines all the functions of a DBMS with some very sophisticated, simple to use tools. These tools are normally called the "Front End" as they form the interface between you the user and the DBMS.

One of the basic communications options is via SQL (Structured Query Language). SQL is a simple method of talking to the database without using the menu systems and is far more flexible.

We will not be covering SQL in this book, as it would double its size. All the data retrievals, updates, deletions, etc. that we are going to cover in the book can be done using SQL, and more besides. We will concentrate on the user interfaces that can be used without learning another programming language. These tools are often referred to as **Visual Programming** tools.

1.4.2 Before INGRES Release 6

Prior to INGRES Release 6 there were other versions, not surprisingly ranging from 1 to 5. We will only be concerned with Release 6 in this book, and all the exercises are based on the Release 6 features. Earlier releases can be used with this book, but if your machine complains about something that you have told it to do don't worry. You will find that most of the tools behave in much the same way, and a little cunning can get you out of most difficulties.

1.4.3 Release 6 and beyond

Release 6 is the latest version of INGRES and has a significant number of differences from earlier releases. One of the major advantages that release 6 has over earlier releases is the ease with which new tools can be added to the basic release.

Latest amongst these are the Knowledge Manager and INGRES/Windows 4GL. The Knowledge Manager alows the embedding of rules in the database. For example if you want to prevent a user from deleting department details if there are still members of that department on file, use a rule. This would previously have been catered for by a program, but the rule is global and is a part of the data, not a feature of any program.

The INGRES/Windows 4GL opens the user to the world of windows based programming and applications. Anyone who has used a windows based system, like a Apple Macintosh or a Sun workstation, will appreciate the advantages immediately. INGRES/Windows 4GL allows the applications programmer to develop applications that are easy to use, and very powerful, but up to ten times faster to develop than ordinary 4GL applications.

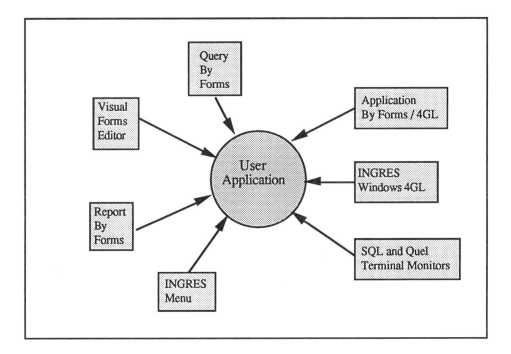

Figure 1.8 INGRES user interfaces

Even as I am writing this there are teams of engineers and designers working away to make this book out of date. This should not be of concern, unless you are reading this in an antique book shop in 23rd century Antarctica. The basic functionality may be getting better, but it will still be recognizable for some time to come. So on with the rest of the book and enjoy yourself, because this should be fun.

1.5 Chapter Review

During this chapter you have been introduced to the organization of the book, and how to progress through the exercises.

There have been some brief discussions on the fundamentals of databases, relational databases and INGRES in particular.

You have also covered

o   Joins

o   Projections

o   Views

o   Tables

o   Rows

o   Columns

These concepts will be used throughout the book. Should you feel that you don't understand a term, then the glossary at the back of the book can probably help you. Remember, if you really get stuck, the magic phrase "Beam me up Scotty". This will only work if your communicator is turned on!

Chapter 2

Database Design

2.1 Introduction

This chapter can be missed entirely if you have experience in designing databases, or you are more interested in working with the visual programming tools. It is included here for completeness, but is not essential to an understanding of INGRES. A database schema and further information is available in Appendix A. This chapter sees us start examining the mysteries of recognizing and defining problems and some methods used to solve those problems. Its main purpose is to demonstrate and discuss some methods used to develop a database design. We will use the examples and exercises in this chapter to develop a simple database that can be used in all of the subsequent chapters.

Database and applications software can be regarded as a major part of a solution to a problem. Before we look at a solution we must first define the problem, which we do in section 2.2.

One of the keys to business efficiency is fast, accurate information in an easily digestible form. This provides an accurate platform for decision making. Computer databases have been developing as an effective way of collecting, collating and finally distributing information. As this book is about the INGRES tools, it should not be hard to decide what database management system we are going to use.

2.2 The Problem

As an example for this chapter and the rest of the book we are going to apply INGRES to a problem experienced by a fictional small company "ABC Supplies". ABC provides office services, supplies and stationery. Customers telephone ABC with orders, problems and complaints, but also with requests for information. Orders are noted and passed on to ABC's order processing department. Information requests and complaints are dealt with mainly by the employee who answers the call. Customers' telephone requests have been mislaid, in the past, leading to complaints. To promote a professional approach it has been decided to use computers to log telephone calls. If this proves successful automated order processing would also be a requirement. As the managing director said in an interview:

> "At the moment all we are looking for is some way of logging customer calls. We need to know who called when, and what equipment or service they called about. We also need to know who took the call. Once we have that information we want to know what action has been taken, by whom, but most important of all we don't want to lose any details."

A problem, simply stated, could still result in analysis taking a number of man/years to complete. It would be impractical in this book to devote a great deal of time to such an analysis; such techniques are well documented elsewhere. However it must be stressed that an effective problem and requirement analysis is a major building block for any system. This provides a full and complete understanding of any problem. You should remember that you cannot build tall buildings on bad foundations.

This chapter describes some relational database design techniques and applies them to the "ABC Supplies" problem for illustration. The case study has some intentional omissions, such as order processing, but the examples are sufficiently detailed to allow for construction of a working telephone call logging database. Modifications can be made to make this fit "real world" problems.

2.3 Methodologies

There are many methods and standards available to the professional analyst and designer, such as Yourdon, Demarco, SSADM or LSDM. This chapter does not describe any of these methods, as they require a book each. Parts of these techniques can be detected in the more simplistic technique outlined in this chapter. An important point, however, is that these techniques may be simple, but they are still effective.

There are two basic approaches in any method and these are used as a starting point for our design. The **top down** approach establishes what is wanted from the system. Once the job that the system is going to do is understood then the data used and stored will be self explanatory. For example, if you know that the system will need to print a list of the customers' names and addresses, then obviously some of the data needs to be customer names and addresses.

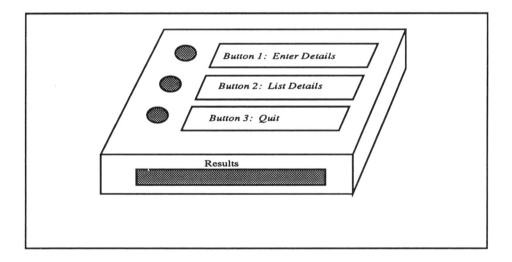

Figure 2.1 "Black box" computing

Bottom up methods first establish the data needed to be manipulated and the processing then becomes obvious. An example to illustrate this approach could be if you are holding equipment details, then there must be some way of entering, changing or deleting those details.

A judicious mixture of these approaches can be used. It goes without saying that an exhaustive analysis of problems and requirements is a precursor to all design solutions. It is normally held as good practice to complete the analysis before embarking on design. This rule of thumb has often been ignored, with sometimes disastrous results.

2.3.1 Top down

Not knowing where to start is always a problem so to start with the top down methods try to think about the computer as a black box. On this black box you can create a number of buttons which represent the functions of the system, as shown in Figure 2.1. To select any of these

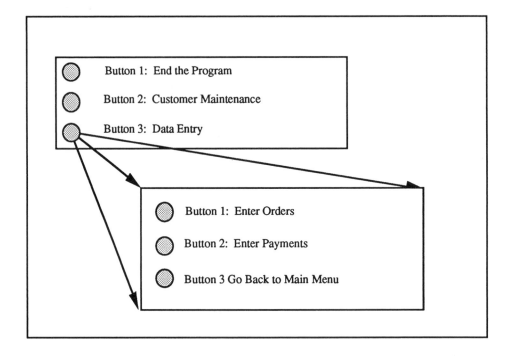

Figure 2.2 Menu hierarchy

functions, you just need to press the button next to the function, and see the results come out.

To start designing our sample database we should define all the functions needed, by adding buttons and labelling them. Once the buttons have been defined they should be reviewed and moved into functional groups, for example, all the reports would be in one functional group, unless you decided to group the management reports separately. Depending on the problem you could also group all the data entry buttons together. These functional groups then become buttons or functions themselves. This gives you a menu hierarchy as shown in Figure 2.2.

Eventually we arrive at a situation where each "button" describes a single function. A single function could be "Add a customer's name and address to the database". This function may contain a number of steps. The steps shown in Figure 2.3 give some idea of the breakdown of functions into steps. We do not need to examine all the steps in a function, at the moment, as some of these steps can be automatic in INGRES.

Function: Add a customer's name and address to the database.

> **Step 1** Check that this is a new customer, and exit if it is not.
>
> **Step 2** Enter the customer's details to the screen
>
> **Step 3** Check the customer's details are correct
>
> **Step 4** Write the customer's details to the file
>
> **Step 5** Are there any more customer's? Exit if there are not.

Figure 2.3 Add customer details function

2.3.2 Bottom up

Bottom up design is basically an attempt to define data used in an organization, and from this design the processes needed to manipulate that data. A common starting point is to describe and draw out the reports you wish to generate. In an existing system these reports may be available to you. A rough draft of the layout and the data needed can lead on refinement to a complete and accurate data model of the data for that report. Further decisions on what data is going to be put into the system, and what screen displays will be used, will further refine the data model, until it is time to decide on the processing required.

Here is a point where we diverge from relational theory, which would normally guide us. Relational theory states that anything that can be calculated from the database files should not be held in file storage. Subtotals and grand totals of prices for example are calculated from the values of data held on file and need not be held in the database. These totals and other values can be calculated by a report program. This approach is fine for values that are infrequently used, and leads to efficient use of the storage space. This leads to a compact database, but can bring other problems that the designer should be aware of. The following example is a cautionary tale of potential disaster to be avoided.

To calculate the number of current employees a computer can be instructed to read the employees' files and add up the number of current employees. Simple, is it not? Especially as a computer can count far faster than a human. However, here comes the snag: this reading of the employees' file, line by line, must be done every time that you need that number. Just think, every time that you need a number for the employees' in a department, a region, or the company, you need to read the employees' file line by line. With 50 employees this is a trivial task, but when your company grows to 5000 employees this may introduce a significant time delay. A simple workaround is to hold the number of employees on file, and use this number rather than reading the file each time. Still, as my old grandma said, 'Nothing in this world is free'. The problem of this workaround revolves around the accuracy of the database. Once you add or delete an employee, or even move the employee into another department you have to change the totals held on file. Data integrity can be very important and this sort of work around can compromise it. Be careful in these circumstances.

From this example you can see simple changes may have more implications than you first thought. For each change you make to a database data model you should weigh the implications, such as the effect on storage requirements and speed of retrieval. In the above case storage efficiency is traded against more work for the developer. A fundamental error detected and resolved early in design can save a fortune in time and money.

2.3.3 Normalization

In reality normalization is a part of bottom up data analysis, but it deserves a separate mention because of its importance. Normalization is a technique, developed by Codd, for the decomposition of complex data structures into flat files.

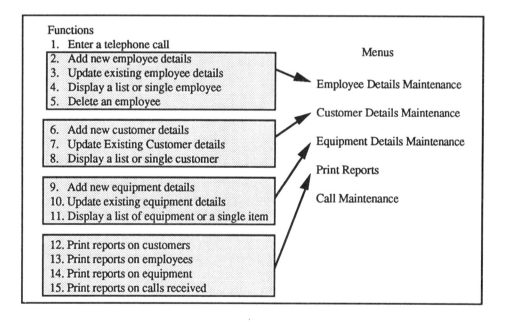

Figure 2.4 Grouping functions into menus

This is a stage by stage process, capable of mathematical accuracy. The stages produce what are called **First, Second** and **Third Normal Form,** hence normalization. A list of data required, with all the data items, is called **un-normalized** data. A unique identifier for the data, an invoice number, for example would be noted. A group of repeating,

identical types of data, for example, lines on an invoice on an un-
normalized form, would be moved to a separate group. This splitting out
of repeating types of data would produce a number of groups of data, and
these are said to be in **First Normal Form**. This technique is built on
by two further steps, and eventually produces data in **Third Normal
Form**. There are other normal forms of data, but for practical purposes
third normal form presents the best logical view of the data.

The data designs produced are compact and efficient, with very
little redundancy. Data redundancy occurs where the same item of data is
held in more than one place in the database, for example the name of a
piece of equipment held in three or four different places. Normalized
databases are easy to maintain and modify, but a full description of the
technique, involving removing repeating groups, resolving partial key
dependencies and partial data dependencies, is outside the scope of this
book. Normalization is a useful technique to use if you are going to be
involved in large and complex projects. Parts of the normalization
process are considered later in the chapter.

2.4   The ABC Supplies Solution: Top Down

In this section we discuss the application of the first technique, top down,
to the ABC supplies problem. Remember to start top down by deciding on
the functions that you are going to use, and making a list of them. Before
noting all the functions or button labels and drawing reports it is best to
make sure that you have a clear idea of the problem. Have another look at
section 2.2, the problem, before going any further, if you are not sure
on any points. I agree that it is a sketchy brief, but that is as good as it
gets.

From reviewing the problem it should be obvious that a key
function of the system will be telephone call logging. Make this the first
function recorded. Since we would also be dealing with customers we
need some method of registering or entering customer details. Employee
lists will tell us who is employed in the company. Equipment details are
part of a customer's purchases. These could complete an overall picture
and be used to build up the list of functions on the left-hand side of
Figure 2.4.

As you can see from Figure 2.4 the first five functions can be
grouped into one overall function called **Employee Details**

Maintenance. Maintenance in this context signifies the addition, modification and deletion of data. This grouping process can be continued for each of the other functions and would result in a main menu, looking like the right-hand side of Figure 2.4.

Exercise 2.1

Expand the list for each report by making information implied in a general report more specific. For example :

Print reports on customers can be expanded to:

12.1   Print report on customers grouped by equipment.
12.2   Print report on customers grouped by calls recieved.
12.3   Print report on a single customer.
12.4   Print report of all customers' names and addresses.

The prefix 12, above, refers to the function originally specified. Use numbering schemes like this to help you keep your place in a complex task.

Appendix A contains more details so if you have no time to carry out this exercise, don't worry as you can use the outline system in Appendix A.

2.5 The ABC Supplies Problem: Bottom Up

Once the functionality of the system has been outlined it is time to look at the data model. With experience you will find that top down and bottom up techniques will run in parallel, neither one comes first. The data can mostly be defined by looking at the output of the system. Output is generally defined as printed reports, screen displays and also includes invoices, mailing labels and mailshots. In an existing system you may already have examples of these. Output can be grouped generically as reports. This term will be used throughout the remainder of the book. As an example we will look at the customer list report. This simple report will define the technique used to discover some of the data to be held in the system for this report to be produced

		Customer Name and Address List		
		List prepared on April 28 1990		
Cust No	Contact Name	Customer Name	Customer Address	Billing Code
233	B. Smith	Smith Ltd	Unit 23 Hounslow Rd	C1
243	R. Jones	JLJ Ltd	1232 Wilson St	B1
59	Sam Wong	Wong Importers	Lotus House, Aylesbury, Bucks	C2
472	Jack Jones	Tomlin & Jones	48 Castle Street, High Wycombe, Bucks	E3

Figure 2.5 Customer name and address report

Stage 1 of this process is to draw up the report. The example in Figure 2.5 shows a typical report that may already exist in the company. Normalization would be the classic technique to apply at this stage. The method that we use is more rough and ready, but in small systems will work as well.

The next stage is to draw up a list of the data on the report, ignoring page numbers and date of the report. Page numbers and dates are generated by the computer and are not necessarily data that you would hold in the system. The report column headings are useful guidelines to deciding what data is being shown. Figure 2.6 gives a list of the data from the report in Figure 2.5. The other part of this step is to list where the data has come from.

As you can see from Figure 2.6 some of the data will be held in the database files, for example customer name and address. Some may be entered at the time the report is generated, time and date for example. Any data input at report time, perhaps used as selection criteria, is called raw data. This needs to be noted, but not held on file. As previously mentioned, anything that can be calculated from data already held on file may not be held itself.

Data Object	Object Source
List Prepared Date	Generated by the System
Customer Number	From Customer File
Contact Name	From Customer File
Customer Name	From Customer File
Customer Address	From Customer File
Billing Details	From Customer File
Total Number	Calculated by Report Program

Figure 2.6 List of data from customer list report

Exercise 2.2

Using the report layout in Figure 2.7, create a list of data needed for the report, and also where the data are held or created. Do not worry if you have an incomplete list containing items like "all the customers on file", as this type of item will be resolved later in the design.

If you have time, and wish to reinforce these techniques, draw up draft formats for all the reports you identified in Exercise 2.1, and list the data needed. A more comprehensive list of the data is included in Appendix A.

Some reports require more than one list of data for completion, for example, customers grouped by calls received would need a list of customers to be matched with a list of calls received.

2.6 Tables, Rows, Columns and Joins - Revisited

As already mentioned in the previous chapter, relational databases are made up of tables of related data, with each column containing a distinct type of data, and each row containing one value for each of the columns in the table.

```
Equipment Customers Report                    Report prepared on April 28th 1989

Equipment: Electronic typewriter type J37B

Cust      Contact      Customer     Customer                      Billing
No.       Name         Name         Address                       Code

233       B.Smith      Smith Ltd    Unit 23, Hounslow Rd Hayes    C1
243       R.Jones      JLJ Ltd      1223 Wilson St                B3
                                    .......
                                    .......
155       I.Kahn       Kahn Bros    12 Heath Rd, Kingston         C2

Total Customers for this equipment  23


                      -------------------
Equipment: Four Drawer filing cabinet

Cust      Contact      Customer     Customer                      Billing
No.       Name         Name         Address                       Code

233       B.Smith      Smith Ltd    Unit 23, Hounslow Rd Hayes    C1
247       C.Ray        WR Moulds    44 Beak Street EC2            B7
                                    .......
                                    .......
243       R.Jones      JLJ Ltd      1223 Wilson St                B2

Total Customers for this equipment  23
```

Figure 2.7 Equipment/customer report

Holding the customer address in one column means making space available for the longest possible address, as well as the shortest address. Many addresses may be shorter than the longest address in the system. This could cause a waste of expensive disk storage. In a small table this is a trivial concern. However consider that in the lifetime of a database 25 rows in a table, possibly wasting 100 bytes of storage, could become 25000 rows, wasting 100000 bytes of storage. It is also true that large tables of data take time to read. These are not unusual volumes of data in a commercial database.

Customer List Table		
Customer Reference	Customer Name	Customer Address
233	Smiths Ltd	Unit 23, Hounslow Rd, Hayes, Middlesex
247	WR Moulds	44 Beak Street EC2
243	JLJ Ltd	1223 Wilson Street, Catford, Essex
155	Kahn Bros	Prospect Building, 12 Heath Road, Kingston upon Thames, Surrey

Figure 2.8 Customer list table

Using the concept of a join, linking small tables together by defining common columns, we can overcome this problem. If you are unsure about the concept of joins, re-read the appropriate section of the introductory chapter. An example based on the customer list table in Figure 2.8 may help.

Customer Reference	Customer Name	Customer Address Line1	Customer Address Line 2	Customer Address Line3	Customer Address Line4

Figure 2.9 Separated address lines

First separate the customer address into a number of smaller columns, address line 1, address line 2, address line 3, as in Figure 2.9.

This may look as though it has made things worse, as we now have to have the maximum number of columns (perhaps as many as six) to hold the longest address. We have potentially an even greater wastage, as space may be wasted in each unused column.This brings us onto the next step.

Remove the repeating group of addresses, and create a separate table that contains only address lines and reference numbers. A repeating group is a group of more than one column that hold the same data. For example we have four address lines, each holding address type data. It may also be necessary to introduce another element to the key, such as line number to place each line in the right order. I have left this out for brevity. Figure 2.10 shows the end result of this step.

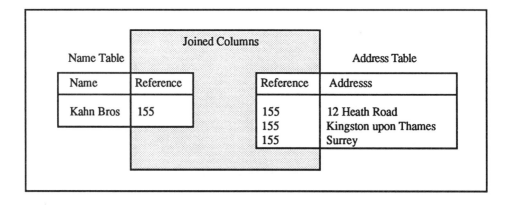

Figure 2.10 Two table join

The final step is to establish a column in both tables which holds **common** values, to allow extraction of common information by using a join. It is important to remember that if there is no match between values in the tables then no row will be retrieved. A join of the tables in Figure 2.10 would result in the output shown in Figure 2.11.

Notice how the reference is the same for the related address data. We could add many more rows of address information. As long as all this information has the same reference number it will be extracted in a join. We now have the flexibility to add as many address lines as we need and also reduce wasted space. This is a common technique and the data structures, or tables, produced are said to be in first normal form.

Reference	Name	Address
155	Kahn Bros	12 Heath Rd Kingston upon Thames Surrey

Figure 2.11 Join result

Exercise 2.3

Examine the lists of data produced as a result of Exercise 2.2 and look for repeating groups. Use the technique described above to help you identify and remove the repeating groups, moving them to groups of their own.

2.7 Three or More Table Joins

There is no restriction on the number of tables that can be joined together; all they need are similar columns. Figure 2.12 describes a join between the equipment, customer and order tables. The join is a link between equipment and order based on the equipment number. The other part of the join is a link between order and customer address tables with the join being provided by the reference column.

The columns that have matching names usually have matching types of data; this is not always so, but is normal practice. In general table and column names should be descriptive. This is another of the strengths of the relational model. Remember, it is easy to see that the age column in the employee file will hold the employee age values. It is more difficult to establish what is held in column ER_PD_3 in ER_MAS_2 table! Joins will feature in other parts of the book.

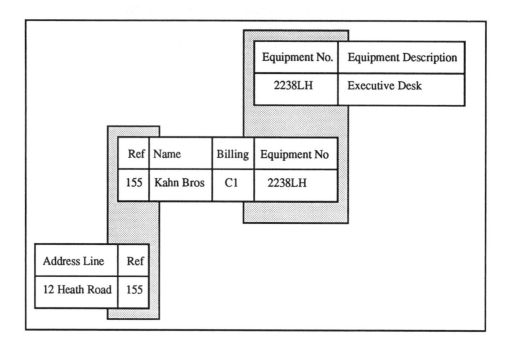

Figure 2.12 Three table join

2.8 Database Schema Design

It should now be possible with the armoury of skills described to design the schema of the call logging database. A schema is the term used to describe a map of the overall logical structure of a database. A relational database consists of tables and processes, therefore its schema would contain table descriptions, and descriptions of the processes that manipulate that data. So far we have been working with logical data; now we must design the physical database, and the physical processes using it.

2.8.1 Table design

The first step in table design is to examine the lists of data that have been compiled from report layouts, and extra data that may be needed. If these lists contain vague entries, i.e. all equipment on file, now is the time to decide how to expand this list into its component parts. Equipment name, equipment cost and number in stock would all be grouped in an equipment file. Once this has been done for all the lists of data they should be checked to establish what relationships they have with each other, and what relationships their group has with other groups. If you are unsure of the need for these relationships, re-read the introduction, and the previous section on joins, etc. Any data item whose place or relationship you are unsure about, place on one side; only group the obvious items as in Figure 2.13.

There may be some other data that need storage, but are not obviously parts of existing groups. Billing Code for example, is this a feature of the customer group or the cost of equipment? The strength of the relational model in allowing changes to be made can be used to advantage in this case. Make a decision on the extra data, include them in groups, discuss their functions within those groups, and carry out a speculative exercise. "What if I made billing code a part of the equipment table, what would it contain, and are its contents appropriate to this group?" Decisions can always be changed, but it is best to get the design right at the start.

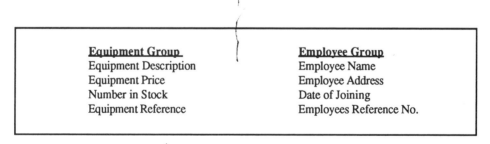

Equipment Group	**Employee Group**
Equipment Description	Employee Name
Equipment Price	Employee Address
Number in Stock	Date of Joining
Equipment Reference	Employees Reference No.

Figure 2.13 Item grouping

With the data grouped together, and vague items now allocated to groups, it is time to review the groups. If possible do this with a colleague. They may ask questions which are difficult to answer, highlighting a problem area in your solution. In this case perhaps a change in design is needed. Colleagues can focus on items possibly ignored or forgotten in your design. Remember "Two heads are better than one".

2.8.2 Surrogate keys

As you can see there are two new items in the groups in Figure 2.15, equipment reference and employee reference. This is a common technique to ensure uniqueness of the rows in the database. It is most common where the key of a database table is larger than 40 per cent of the row size, or the key values are not in themselves unique. The 40 per cent figure is a guideline used on INGRES tables. When tables have indexes, to enable fast access, part of the index contains the key. It is often the case that the key is stored twice, once in the data and once in the index. This can result in an increase in storage space, therefore an alternative, shorter key may solve this problem.

Imagine a name and address table keyed on surname. There are 14 pages of Smith in the London telephone directory. How do you distinguish them? Surname alone is not good enough. First name? There are three pages of John Smith. From this you can see that referring to a short, arbitrary, unique key, a reference number perhaps, would be more concise and accurate. This is called a surrogate key.

2.8.3 Joins and keys

Examine the functionality that you require from the system. With this functionality in mind ask yourself, for each report, "Which groups need to be joined together, and what are the items on which they join?" If groups are to be joined check for common columns on which they can be joined. If the columns are missing you have to include them. The best way to do this is to compare tables. The table that has the largest number of rows for a unique value, like the **address** table in Figure 2.10, is called a **subordinate** group. Take the common value, in this case **address**

reference, and make sure it is stored in the major group, the **name** table.

For example, the equipment group in Figure 2.14 has a unique identifier, equipment reference. The call details group has a unique identifier, call reference. However to establish the relationship between calls that are coming in and the equipment that the calls are about, it is necessary to include an equipment reference in the call details group.

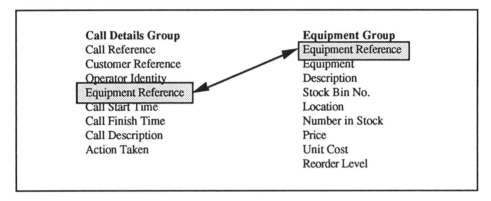

Figure 2.14 Common columns

This reference, which is not unique in call details, but is the unique key in equipment details, makes a join possible between the two tables. Equipment reference in the call details group is called a foreign key. A foreign key is a column in a table that is not the key to that table, but a key to another table.

2.8.4 Database table descriptions

Database table descriptions contain a list of the column names and the storage formats of the data. The column name must be unique within a table description, but not within a database. The pairing of the table name and column name must be unique. It is sufficient for the moment to know that the groups described are going to become the table descriptions for this database.

Exercise 2.4

Draw up a complete list of groups of data and their contents. Establish joins between groups using surrogate keys and foreign keys.

2.9 Forms Design

Now that you have a good idea about the data that is going to be part of the database, it is time to design screen forms for collecting that data. Screen form designs are used as the input to Chapter 6 on VIFRED. Simple forms for single tables can be easily designed, as in Figure 2.15. This is a form to add a single employee to the employee table. Each of the columns in the employee table is available for input on the screen.

```
┌─────────────────────────────────────────────────────────────┐
│                                                               │
│                  Employee File Maintenance                    │
│                                                               │
│                      Add an Employee                          │
│                                                               │
│                                                               │
│          Employee Name           _____          │
│                                                               │
│          Employee Charge Rate    _____          │
│                                                               │
│          Personnel Number        _____          │
│                                                               │
│          Operator ID             _____          │
│                                                               │
└─────────────────────────────────────────────────────────────┘
```

Figure 2.15 Employee form

More complex forms may be needed for joined tables. These are typical if there is a one to many relationship between the two tables. This is where one row of a table is joined to many rows of another table. Entering a call would join the call group to the call details group, where an operator may be entering information about one or more pieces of equipment in one call. Figure 2.16 shows a form for a one to many, or master to detail join. In this case a call will be entered for one or many pieces of equipment. Since Call ID is common to both the call and call details table it is entered only once, at the top of the form.

This is called a master/detail join. One set of data is static once entered, and a number of lines entered related to the static data.

Reports are simply forms that display data, with no data entry capability, but are designed in the same way as ordinary forms.

Exercise 2.5

Use your list of groups and the list of functionality to design a number of forms for the data entry. Do not spend too much time designing the exact layout; this can be done interactively during the VIFRED exercises.

Call Details Entry

Call ID
Customer No
Operator ID
Start Time
Finish Time

Equipment ID	Call Description	Action

Figure 2.16 Call details form

2.10 Chapter Review

At the end of this chapter we have covered the following techniques:

o   Describe a problem in simple terms by listing functions and operations that solve the problem.

o   Group the operations into main menu items and submenus.

o   Draft report layouts and identify data required.

o   Group data into tables.

o   Relate tables of data to each other using primary keys, foreign keys and surrogate keys.

o   Design data entry, display forms and reports.

Chapter 3

Getting Started

3.1 Createdb - A Command for Creating Databases

When you have completed the analysis and design stages it's time to get your hands on INGRES. It is time to build a database and populate it with tables. This chapter help you to create a database, add tables and specify data storage formats.

First a note from our sponsor (PC users can ignore the next paragraph).

On a multi-user computer you will need to be "registered" as an INGRES user as well as having a user login ID. INGRES permissions must be set to allow you to create databases. All of these are done for you, by the system and database administrators. Contact your system administrator, and INGRES installation administrator, who will execute the necessary program. On a standalone PC this step is not necessary. (Check Appendix G for other differences between PC INGRES and multiuser INGRES.)

From now on we will assume that you are sitting at a terminal, ready to start working with INGRES. This is the best way to learn and make the mistakes that re-inforce learning! All the exercises in this chapter are practical, and require access to a terminal or PC. Try to temper enthusiasm with caution. The exercises are staged to allow you easily to build up a database with tables. Don't try to go too far too fast and make things more difficult for yourself.

3.1.1 Operating system commands.

Starting to work with a database is very simple, using a menu system, and simple commands, but before you can use the menu system you will need a database to work on. This is simple to achieve. With a terminal displaying a system prompt, for example,

```
$>
```

type in the command to create a database.

```
$> createdb fred
```

This command is separated from the parameter fred by a space. You could use any legal name to create a database (see section on names below), but before you try the exercise, a little on what createdb does.

3.1.2 What does createdb do and where?

Createdb creates sub directories and empty tables by copying templates into a default location. To find the default location check the symbol or environment variable II_DATABASE. Your system administrator can tell you how to do this. These directories and tables are called system catalogs, and make up the INGRES data dictionary. The data dictionary stores specifications for the tables, forms, reports and queries that are part of that database (these are called database "objects"). To find out more about the contents of the data dictionary you need to use SQL commands. For further information on system catalogs and other objects look in the database administrator's guide for your system.

3.1.3 Database naming

Database names can be composed of up to 24 characters, but the first eight characters should be unique. This is due to some operating systems truncating names to eight characters. You can use numbers, letters and the underscore. Stick to lower case as this saves problems if you move the database to another machine that is case sensitive. If you have a company standards manual that may help you with naming conventions.

Try and make the name meaningful. In the example above a database called "fred" gives no hint as to its contents. Some system design methods give really meaningful names like oldb23_q1_89. There, that was an easy database name, instantly translatable (on-line database number 23, for first quarter of 1989). Names for development should be short and meaningful, salesaccs, or course_mgmt. This is the start of the creative art of computing.

3.1.4 Command line flags

The createdb command has a number of flags which give more flexibility and power. A flag is a word or phrase added to a command which changes the way in which the command works. Flags are always preceded by a hyphen, and sometimes followed by a parameter. There are two useful flags for the createdb command:

-p   Creates a private database, which is hidden from other users.

-u   Allows the INGRES superuser to impersonate the named user, and creates a database owned by that user.

The following two examples demonstrate how the flags are used. The effect of the flags is explained in the text below them.

```
createdb -p salesbook
```

creates a private database called salesbook. No other user can view or gain access to objects in this database, unless they are given permission. Also users cannot create tables or other objects in this type of database without permission.

```
createdb -usamuels stock
```

creates a database called stock, which is owned by the user samuels. There is no space between the flag and the parameter, samuels. This also makes samuels the database administrator of stock.

Exercise 3.1 Creating a database

Make sure you are a legitimate INGRES user before attempting this exercise. All exercises from now on make this assumption. If you are unsure ask your system administrator. This does not apply to users of PC INGRES.

From the operating system prompt create a database called "exercise", or exer_CC, replacing CC with your initials. You must use an underscore rather than a hyphen to separate letters. This is good if there is more than one of you following this book. You will not need any command line flags for this. Wait until the computer has returned the prompt before continuing. If you are feeling confident try typing "catalogdb exercise" at the operating system prompt. (If you get into trouble pressing the PF4 function key will usually return to the operating system, or a previous menu.)

3.2 Ingmenu - The INGRES Main Menu

Ingmenu is a menuing system that will allow you to move between menu frames, carrying out complex operations without entering operating system commands, or exiting to operating system level. Although all the INGRES sub systems like Vifred, the visual forms editor, can be entered directly from the operating system, you cannot subsequently take an option to start Ingmenu without moving to operating system level. All the important INGRES operations are available from Ingmenu. Mastering the style of Ingmenu is important as all the other menu driven options behave in a similar way. All of the INGRES Menus, even ones you will create yourself, use function keys "attached" to menu options. These are usually shown in brackets after the menu choice, e.g. Forms (F11). To take the menu option press either the function key or escape followed by the menu name and return. I have not shown the menu function keys on the figures in the book to help a little with clarity. Keys change according to the type of terminal used. So missing them off the illustrations will make the illustrations more general.

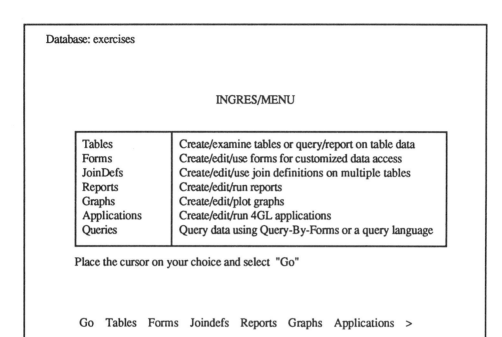

Figure 3.1 Ingmenu

3.2.1 How to start ingmenu

The most straightforward way of manipulating data is to use the INGRES Menu system. This provides an easy, menu driven interface with the INGRES subsystems. To start the INGRES menu systems type:

```
ingmenu <dbname>
```

This will start a front end and link this with the server. A server is equivalent to the database manager. If no server is present then an error message is displayed. When ingmenu has finished operating, the screen will look like Figure 3.1.

3.2.2 Moving around the system and making selections

INGRES frames include menus of operations and windows for displaying forms and data. A frame in INGRES means a screen form and some functions. The menu frame in Figure 3.1 is a good example. The screen form tells you what you can do, the menu line tells you how to do it.

```
Database: exercises



                            INGRES/MENU


       ┌─────────────┬──────────────────────────────────────────────┐
       │ Tables      │ Create/examine tables or query/report on table data │
       │ Forms       │ Create/edit/use forms for customized data access │
       │ JoinDefs    │ Create/edit/use join definitions on multiple tables │
       │ Reports     │ Create/edit/run reports                        │
       │ Graphs      │ Create/edit/plot graphs                        │
       │ Applications│ Create/edit/run 4GL applications               │
       │ Queries     │ Query data using Query-By-Forms or a query language │
       └─────────────┴──────────────────────────────────────────────┘



     WhatToDo (PF1)    Keys(F11)    Field(F12)    Help(F13)    End(PF3)
```

Figure 3.2 Online help menu

Other messages may be placed on your screen, error messages, program messages, etc. (even broadcast messages to say the machine is being closed down!), however the methods of controlling these messages is outside the scope of this book. All INGRES forms behave in the same way, with a menu line at the bottom of the screen, from which you make selection of an operation, and a forms window for further interaction with the data. Some menu lines are at the top of the screen, PC INGRES will let you specify this, to make PC INGRES look and feel more like popular PC software.

You can cycle through the menu options by pressing the menu key. A "right arrow" >, or a "left arrow" <, indicates that there are more menu selections "off" screen. To locate the menu key, ask your system administrator (if they are not in the office, try the nearest bar). The keyboard mapping, a description of keys and their functions, can also be obtained from the INGRES Forms Menus and Report Writer Manual.

WhatToDo	Decribes the current screen and the operations menu.
Keys	Describes the function control keys and the current definition. If you can't remember what keys perform actions like moving backwards through fields in the window, this is where they are listed.
Field	This option is not always available, but tells you about the field, validation, dataformat, etc. when it is present.
Help	Tells you what help is available.
End	Exits from help screen to the previous screen.

Figure 3.3 Help options

When an INGRES frame is displayed the cursor is placed on the data window or the menu line. If the cursor is on the menu line it is possible to make your selection by typing in the command, usually only the first few letters will do. INGRES will then take the option selected.

To make a selection from the operations when the cursor is on the data window press the associated function key. In Figure 3.2 pressing the key associated with the operation Help(F13), typical of a vt220 keyboard mapping, will invoke help. It is normal to get a "submenu", that is a menu that acts on the current frame giving added options, when selecting help. As you can see from Figure 3.2 the window remains the same but some

```
┌─────────────────────────────────────────────────────────────────┐
│  TABLES - Tables Catalog                                          │
│         ┌───────────────────────┬──────────────┬─────────┐       │
│         │ Name                  │ Owner        │ Type    │       │
│         ├───────────────────────┼──────────────┼─────────┤       │
│         │ customer              │ peterm       │ table   │       │
│         │ equipment             │ peterm       │ table   │       │
│         │ call_details          │ peterm       │ table   │       │
│         │                       │              │         │       │
│         │                       │              │         │       │
│         │                       │              │         │       │
│         │                       │              │         │       │
│         │                       │              │         │       │
│         │                       │              │         │       │
│         └───────────────────────┴──────────────┴─────────┘       │
│                                                                   │
│     Place cursor on row and select desired operation from menu.   │
│                                                                   │
│                                                                   │
│   Create   Destroy   Examine   Query   Report   Find   Top   Bottom  >  │
└─────────────────────────────────────────────────────────────────┘
```

Figure 3.4 Tables menu

different options can be seen on the menu line. I have put in a
representation of the function key mapping for a vt100f terminal in
Figure 3.2. This will give you an idea of what to expect when you are
working, but I will omit them in subsequent figures. The additional
options give the opportunity to get the extra functions listed in Figure 3.3.
To make a selection from the help menu press the function key associated
with an operation, or type in the operation's first few characters
(selecting help puts the cursor on the menu line). A new window will be
displayed, giving the information requested. To finish with help press the
function key associated with the "end" option.

Exercise 3.2

Invoke INGMENU on your sample database, examine the INGRES main menu system, and use the help option to make yourself familiar with the operations available. Only use help from the main menu; don't make any selections at the moment as that comes later.

3.3 Tables - A Utility to Manipulate Database Tables

3.3.1 Creating tables

To create a table first you must choose the tables option from Ingmenu. You will notice that even though your window may not be the Ingmenu main menu you can still take the tables option. Taking the tables option gives a window that looks like Figure 3.4

To create a table press the function key associated with the create option. Remember that before you can do anything in INGRES the object you want to work with must exist or you must create it. The exercise at the end of the section will help you to create the tables in our sample database. Once the create option has been taken the screen displays a different frame, the **Create a Table** frame. An example is shown in Figure 3.5

Each of the options listed in the create a table frame deals specifically with the create option. However remember that standard operations are available, find, top, bottom, help, etc. The cursor will now be on the first field on the form. This is the table name field. You must have a valid name in this field to create a table. INGRES names must start with a character, be less than 24 characters long, and include only numbers, letters and the underscore character (_). To move off the first field press the tab key, which is the standard INGRES key for moving on to the next field on a form (help, followed by the keys option, will tell you how to move back to the previous field).

Once a name has been put in the table name field pressing tab or return will move the cursor on to the column name section of the frame. This is where you enter the column names that you have decided on in your design. After entering a column name press tab or return to move to the data type field. This is where you enter the internal storage name for the data that you will save in the column you have named. Section 4 contains details on INGRES data types.

```
┌─────────────────────────────────────────────────────────────────┐
│  TABLES - Create a Table                                         │
│                                                                  │
│       Enter the name of the new table    _____     │
│                                                                  │
│       Enter the column specifications of the new table:          │
│    ┌──────────────────┬──────────────┬──────┬───────┬─────────┐  │
│    │ Column Name      │ Data Type    │ Key  │ Nulls │ Defaults│  │
│    │                  │              │      │       │         │  │
│    │                  │              │      │       │         │  │
│    │                  │              │      │       │         │  │
│    │                  │              │      │       │         │  │
│    │                  │              │      │       │         │  │
│    │                  │              │      │       │         │  │
│    │                  │              │      │       │         │  │
│    │                  │              │      │       │         │  │
│    └──────────────────┴──────────────┴──────┴───────┴─────────┘  │
│                                                                  │
│  Insert   Delete   Blank   Move   GetTableDef   Save  Find  Top >│
└─────────────────────────────────────────────────────────────────┘
```

Figure 3.5 Create a table

Whatever you do remember to SAVE YOUR TABLES after you have finished editing. This little tip saves a lot of heartache and tears. Tears make the keys all sticky.

3.3.2 Examining tables

Tables are database objects, and you need to check them from time to time, expecially if you have forgotten your schema. Examining tables and their constituent parts is easy: you select the EXAMINE option on the tables catalog frame. This shows you a display something like Figure 3.7. Don't worry if the number of rows is 0; you have only created the table structure, not the data.

For the moment the only parts that need concern us are owner and table type sections. All the other parts of this display are explained later in the chapter.

Owners are the creators of the database tables, and the owners' names are pulled kicking and screaming from the users file, where INGRES user names and ID's are stored. This section should tell you that the owner is you!

3.3.3 Printing tables

From some systems it is possible to print the descriptions of tables by pressing the F8 key. Check with your system administrator to see if this key will work (it may work, but not in the way you expect!). You can print the table descriptions using SQL, and the help option. This could be an easy alternative, but is not discussed here.

Exercise 3.3

Invoke the create table option giving it a table name that you have decided on, based on your designs from Chapter 2, or the samples in Appendix A. Don't start to add columns to the table, this will be done in the next exercise, after we have examined data types.

3.4 Data types and How to Define Internal Storage Types

To store data in a database, INGRES needs to know what sort of data is being stored. This affects the internal storage mechanisms. Choosing the right data type is important as it can affect storage space and efficiency. The following are the data types common in INGRES, although you can define your own data types. This is not a technique for beginners, however, so we will leave it to TOOLS II - the data types strike back!

3.4.1 Character data types

There are four character data types, c, char, vchar and varchar. Vchar and c are equivalent to the INGRES version 5 data types of the same name. Char and varchar are SQL standard names, so their use is recommended to maintain a standard.

c   The c data type consists of a string of up to 2000 printing ASCII characters. The c data type only allows printable characters. INGRES will ignore blanks when comparing c data type strings. For example **brahms and liszt** will be treated identically to **brahmsandliszt**.

char   The char data type differs from the c data type only by converting the nonprintable characters converted to blanks. This data type is compatible with ANSI SQL.

vchar The vchar data type consists of up to 2000 characters in the ASCII extended set or blanks. All ASCII characters except the NULL character are allowed.

varchar The varchar data type consists of up to 2000 characters in the ASCII extended set or blanks. All ASCII characters are permitted, including nonprintable control characters, for example, the NULL character. A varchar column is defined as varchar(n) where n is the maximum number of characters stored in the column. The varchar data type is compatible with ANSI SQL.

3.4.2 Numeric data types

There are two groups of numeric data types, floating point and integer. These two groups can be further subdivided, depending on the size of numbers that can be held. Integers hold whole numbers and floating point holds numbers with fractions. The following table describes the numeric data types and the size and configuration of the numbers that they contain.

3.4.3 Abstract data types

There are two abstract data types, date and money. The type of data they hold should be self-explanatory. They are called abstract, as they are a special data type, of fixed storage format and using special rules for output and manipulation. The definitions of the date and money data types are as follows.

date   Date holds an absolute date, time, or time intervals. The

Datatype	Will Contain
integer1	1 byte integer from -128 to +127
integer2 or smallint	2 byte integer, from -32,768 to +32,767
integer4 or integer	4 byte integer from -2,147,483,648 to +2,147,483,647
float4	4 byte floating from 8.43 x E -37 to 3.37 x E 38
float8	8 byte floating from 4.19 x E -307 to 1.67 x E 308

Figure 3.6 Numeric Datatypes

date data type can hold any valid date between 1st January 1582 and 31st December 2382. Dates can be displayed according to international conventions, defined by system logicals or environment variables II_DATE_FORMAT and II_TIMEZONE.

money The money data type contains decimal currency data. INGRES provides great flexibility with regard to the money data type, allowing you to adapt the display of the data according to your local currency conventions. This control is effected by environment variables. Your system administrator will tell you what your local variables are set to. The variables to check are **II_MONEY_FORMAT** and **II_DECIMAL**.

3.4.4 Null values

Nullability is an attribute of stored data. Null represents inapplicable or missing data. It is most useful when working with numeric data used in aggregate computations, for example totals or averages. Without null values empty data values are set to zero for numeric data types and blank for character data types. These are not the ASCII NULL characters; it equates to nothing, rather than a definite character.

3.5 Creating Columns - How to Add Columns to the Database

3.5.1 Column names

Now the tedious part is finished, it is time to add some columns to the database table that you have started defining in Exercise 3.3. The first thing to do is to give a column a name. This name should be unique for this table (mind you INGRES won't let you add a duplicate column name in a table.) The name doesn't have to be unique in the database, because the pairing of the table and column names must be unique. Column names follow the general naming conventions that have already been outlined in the section on database naming conventions. This is one of the easy parts. Being concerned about lowering the stress level in the world INGRES have adopted standards that hold through the whole database.

Once you have decided on a name for the column, first think about its suitability. Remember what has been said about "meaningful" names. Obscure mixtures of letters and digits, or unrelated names, may mean something to you, but remember the poor people who inherit your fondness for table columns named after great composers! Relational theory expects that the name of a column should identify the contents of the column. Salestotal should be the name for the sales total column, etc. Boring I know, but it makes life easier later on, for you and your successors.

3.5.2 Choosing a data type

Choosing a data type should be done as carefully as choosing a good meal. Enough and a little bit spare is a good rule here. If a number is going to get close to the limit for integer2 then choose a larger integer, or even a floating point data type.

Choose a vchar or varchar data type if you are likely to have data of widely varying sizes in the column. From now on whenever you read varchar you can assume vchar as well. Don't forget to define varchar/vchar as:

```
varchar(34)
vchar(34)
```

The extra 2 bytes that the varchar data type takes contains length data and the data type is a truly variable length data type.

The char or c data type (I'll use char from now on) is especially good for flags or indicators, as you are likely to test indicators for the contents and not the spaces. Char data types are defined by;

```
char(12)
```

Abstract data types are good for the type of data that they hold. It is important to remember that in most cases it is easier to use the INGRES date handling than to write your own.

If there is not enough space for the money that you are dealing with, then use one of the float data types, that should have enough space for even the richest people.

3.5.3 Keys and indexes

At the moment there is no need to worry about these columns, as they come more into the query planning and optimizing of your database access. These will not prevent data being retrieved, but play an important part in the efficiency with which data is retrieved. You should remember from the introduction that one of the features of a relational database is that rows in a database table can be stored in any order, because they should have a unique key identifier. That is what the key column is for, a number in the key column (1,2, etc.) tells INGRES to sort the data in that column in ascending order. For the moment leave the key column blank by tabbing past.

3.5.4 Nullable columns

As previously mentioned null is a special value that represents unknown or unavailable data. You may think that having an empty field with a null value is the same as having a blank field. Nulls however are ignored when calculating an average, therefore the average is not artificially depressed by the "empty" row counting as zero. In the null column you can enter y or n, allowing or disallowing the column to contain nulls.

3.5.5 Finishing off your table

If you enter more column names than the table on the screen can hold, DON'T PANIC. The "table" on the screen is called a table field, and one of its properties is to scroll rows out of sight at the top of the table when you add more rows than the table looks capable of holding. Moving about the table field is accomplished by arrow keys. (If you can't remember which keys are used re-read the help section above). Table fields will scroll rows at the top if you keep pressing the up arrow. If you particularly want to enter a row in between two other rows place the cursor where you want the row and press the Insert option. After the empty row has opened up you can continue entering column details.

When you are satisfied with the contents of your table you must remember to save it (INGRES is very forgiving, and will ask you if you want to save the table before really letting you lose all your work). Until you take the save option you will not see your table in the system catalogs. Saving adds the table descriptions to the **ii_relation** system catalog.

Exercise 3.4

Add the appropriate columns to the table that you have started to create in exercise above. Use the table definitions designed in Chapter 2. When you have created this table, save it and create the remaining tables that you have designed. Use the table definitions in Appendix A if you have not skipped the design chapter.

3.6 Examine Tables - Looking at What Your Tables Contain

3.6.1 Entering examine tables

Once you have saved a number of tables you may wish to examine them. This is most common after you have returned to your system after a short break. Generally people are quite lazy about keeping documentation up to date and this option helps by listing tables and their structures. It is also possible to use the **printscreen** key option to obtain a hard copy.

The figure for pages tells you how many INGRES data pages are allocated for this table. It is outside the scope of this book to discuss storage structures, performance and other database administration issues. A final word about data pages. Overflow is normal with the default storage structure (the heap). If your storage structure is anything else (btree, hash or isam) overflow may be telling you about a potential performance problem.

3.6.2 Journalling

Journalling is a facility to maintain the integrity of the database up to the last complete transaction. If it is important, for example where you are entering large masses of data between backups, you may find journalling gives you piece of mind, as it keeps a record of every complete transaction between the last backup (in this situation we use the term checkpoint) and the next. In the event that there is a problem with your database, you can restore the last checkpoint and play forward all the recorded journals. This will get you back almost to the position you were in before the "crash". This is a very wide and complex subject, and is beyond the scope of this book.

Exercise 3.5

Examine the tables created in Exercise 3.4, and check for inconsistencies between your design and the tables created.

```
┌─────────────────────────────────────────────────────────────────────┐
│                                                                       │
│  TABLES - Examine a Table                                             │
│                  Information on Table customer                        │
│                                                                       │
│       Owner:  petem                          Table Type:  user table  │
│   Row Width:  118                      Storage Structure:  heap       │
│       Rows:  6                           Pages/Overflow:  1/0         │
│     Columns:  7                            Journalling:  disabled     │
│                                                                       │
│   ┌──────────────────────────────┬────────────┬─────┬──────┬────────┐│
│   │ Column Name                  │ Data Type  │ Key │ Nulls│Defaults││
│   ├──────────────────────────────┼────────────┼─────┼──────┼────────┤│
│   │ custno                       │ integer    │     │ yes  │ no     ││
│   │ contact_name                 │ varchar(20)│     │ yes  │ no     ││
│   │ name                         │ varchar(20)│     │ yes  │ no     ││
│   │ address1                     │ varchar(20)│     │ yes  │ no     ││
│   │ address2                     │ varchar(20)│     │ yes  │ no     ││
│   │ address3                     │ varchar(20)│     │ yes  │ no     ││
│   │ billing_code                 │ char(2)    │     │ yes  │ no     ││
│   └──────────────────────────────┴────────────┴─────┴──────┴────────┘│
│                                                                       │
│    NewTable   Find   Top   Bottom   Help   End                        │
│                                                                       │
└─────────────────────────────────────────────────────────────────────┘
```

Figure 3.7 Examine tables

3.7 Changing Table Descriptions

3.7.1 Change table command, and why INGRES doesn't have one!

A common question about INGRES is "Why can't I just press a button and modify my table? My text field is too small."

Well, the good news is that you can change a table structure, but the bad news is that it will take some effort. When you think about a table, lying there full of data, the last thing it needs is a quick change, especially if it is followed by a lengthy reorganization. Any changes you make to the table structure have to be echoed through the underlying data. I know that you may not have any underlying data, but you could have, and the only way to deal with that is the **SQL** bulk **COPY** command.

This is described later. INGRES also has an operating system command COPYDB. This will copy the whole database for you. More details on this and other commands can be found in the SQL manual. The rest of this section is about changing tables that don't have any data in them.

3.7.2. Modifying tables

Create new table
First off you need to create a new table that is going to be the basis of your changed table. Names like temp or test are easy to identify. Use the create table option and enter a table name in the field on the form. Don't enter any columns yet.

Get your table definition
Use the "GetTableDef" option and when asked for a table name that is going to supply the column give it the name of the table that you want to change.

Make changes to new table
GetTableDef copies the column descriptions into your new table and now you can make changes.

Save your table definition
Save your table definition, and save yourself some angst. This will let you destroy your old table in an atmosphere of calm control.

Destroy your old table - Watch out for data!
After you have saved your new table definition you can destroy the old table with, you've guessed, the DESTROY option. Destroy is house trained so it will ask for confirmation, but from this point you are on your own. Don't destroy a table unless you are sure that it doesn't contain irreplaceable data. Try another way of changing table structures.

Rename your table
Now you are in the position of having a table that has the right structure but the wrong name. Follow this recipe and you will end up with a right table structure and a right name.

Create a table and give it the right name.

GetTableDef the structure of the wrong named table

Save the right structure and name together

Delete the wrong name, right structured table

This method may be convoluted as INGRES refuses to let you have tables of identical names in the same database.

3.7.3 Modifying tables with SQL

The data manipulation language SQL has a bulk copy facility. This can be used to copy data out of a table, destroy the old table, recreate a new table, and populate it with data from the old table. SQL is not a part of this book, but if you need this facility the INGRES manuals will help.

Exercise 3.6

If your tables accurately reflect your design, you can skip this exercise, otherwise modify your tables. Increasing a text field length is a harmless way to practise.

3.8 Chapter Review

In this chapter you will have covered

o   Creating databases

o   Accessing a database using INGRES menu

o   Using the Help menus

o   Moving through the INGRES menuing system

o   Selecting the Tables sub system

o   Creating and saving tables

o   Choosing data types for table columns

3.9 Quick Reference

Creating a database

```
createdb   <databasename>
```

Substitute your own database name for <databasename>

Starting INGRES menu

```
ingmenu   <databasename>
```

Creating a New Table

o   Start INGRES menu on your database

o   Select the **Tables** option from INGRES menu

o   Select **Create** from the tables catalog

o   Enter the name of your **table**

o   Enter the name of your **column**

o   Choose the **data type** for the column

o   Decide on your use of **Nulls**

o   Repeat for each column in your table

o   **Save** your table description

Chapter 4

Simple Data Manipulation

4.1 Introduction

4.1.1 What you will learn from the chapter

This chapter is where all the hard work in the previous chapters pays off! This is where your database so painstakingly designed and created will be populated with data. Relational database theory is moved into practice. This chapter will show you how to put data into and extract data from the database. This is a quick method of data manipulation and it is also the easiest to remember and duplicate. All you will be doing is telling the database what tables you want to manipulate, and how you want to manipulate them.

4.1.2 Query by forms

Query by forms is exactly what it says it is. You QUERY the database by filling in a series of forms on the screen. Query By Forms is a common INGRES term (there are also Report By Forms and Application By Forms). Any data access is called a query, even when you are adding data. This is due to the relational concept of tables. First you must ask a master table, which holds the lists of tables in the database, to find the table you want, and then you can access the table. You will soon get used to thinking in terms of queries that are doing something, and not just asking questions.

4.1.3 Data access with QBF

Query by forms, from now on QBF, will allow you to handle data in many simple and quite complex ways, but for the moment we will concentrate on the simple methods. Having mastered these it is a short step to taking over the world.

4.2. Starting Query by Forms

4.2.1. Straight from the operating system

First, like all good programs QBF is impenetrable to the uninitiated. So step up and pay your fee and you can read this section. To start QBF from the operating system type:

```
> qbf test
```

This assumes that you have a database called test. You haven't? What were you doing in the previous chapter? Come back here after you have created a database called test, and built some tables!

Typing **qbf** followed by the database name, and some optional parameters will show you the **QBF** startup frame, as in Figure 4.1.

4.2.2 Using INGRES menu

Instead of starting **QBF** from the operating system you can use INGRES menu to start **QBF**. After you have started INGRES menu you can access all of the subsystems by selecting them. From INGRES menu the subsystem to select is, wait for it, QBF. Although you will also see a **query** option, leave it for the moment; we will discuss this later, in QBF operating phases.

4.2.3 QBF Startup frame

After a short delay this frame is displayed, and this is finally where it really happens. From this frame you can choose to query single tables, multiple tables joined together, and customised forms working on joined tables or single tables.

Some of these options will be familiar to you. Help and Quit, for example, follow normal INGRES conventions.

QBF - Start-up Frame

Query-By-Forms(QBF) is an interactive interface for adding, deleting, changing and viewing data in your database.

You may get a catalog of QBFNames, Joindefs or Tables in your database to serve as a basis for editing and viewing. In summary, they are:

QBFName -   a name that combines a JoinDef or table name with a
                    form name. QBFNames are created in VIFRED

JoinDef   -   a stored specification of joins between tables, and
                    rules governing how to update data in QBF

Table   -   a table or view in your database

From each of the catalogs, you can browse through names, and choose one to serve as a basis for editing or viewing.

Additional utility commands on this menu are:

Help   -   displays help on QBF and your terminal key functions
Quit   -   leaves QBF

QBFNames   JoinDefs   Tables   Help   Quit

Figure 4.1 QBF startup frame

Exercise 4.1

*Decide on a table that you would like to work on during this chapter. If you can't decide, or are using the database schema from Appendix A, select table cust_details or operator (These are tables which do not depend on other tables for their contents). Start **QBF** on your exercise database.*

4.3 Operating Phases of QBF

There are two phases of operation in QBF: these will give you the option of defining your query, and then executing that query. Before you move on actually to use QBF these concepts must be understood.

4.3.1 Query definition

When QBF is invoked by using the QBF option or the **qbf** command from the operating system you are placed in the first of two operating phases, the query definition phase. This is the place where you give INGRES the details of the query objects that you are going to work with.

To make life simple we will only use the table definition option. More complex query objects are used in following chapters. This option allows us to **target** database tables or views. This is where the expression **query target** comes from. There are two other main types of object that are used:

Joindefs   This term is applied to the definitions of the ways that tables are joined together. Joindef, easy isn't it?

QBFnames   This term is used for the customized forms that we will create later and associate with tables and Joindefs.

4.3.2 Query execution

After you have defined your query target you can enter the query execution phase. This will allow you to append or add data to a table, retrieve or view data, and finally update or change data in your table. Where is the delete option I hear you ask? Well, a delete is a change to the existing data (you can't get rid of something that isn't there), so the delete option is part of the update operation.

An important point to note for later. When you choose **retrieve** you won't be able to change the data displayed; you can only do that during **update** or **append**.

4.4 Tables Catalog

The tables catalog is displayed after you select tables from the QBF startup frame. This is where you select a table to work on. This is the list of tables that have been created in your database, although some of these are tables that you may not own.

TABLES - Tables Catalog

Name	Owner	Type
customer	petem	table
equipment	petem	table

Place cursor on row and select desired operation from menu.

Create   Destroy   Examine   Query   Report   >

Figure 4.2 Tables catalog

4.4.1 Catalog contents

The contents of the tables catalog include tables and views, and the owner of the table is shown. Moving about the tables catalog is the same as moving about any INGRES table. Use the help option if you are not sure which keys can be used to move up and down in a table field.

4.4.2 Create, destroy and examine tables

Like much of INGRES, you may wish to include a new table, or remove an old table. Returning from the QBF option to INGRES menu and choosing a tables utility would be wasteful in time and computer resources, so the INGRES tables utility is brought to you in the tables catalog, and selection of **create**, **examine** and **destroy** gives you the same powers as the tables utility used in the previous chapter.

4.4.3 Go or execute

Go on this frame takes you from the QBF definition phase to the QBF execution phase. The parameter given to INGRES as the query target is the table name under the cursor when you select **Go**. Therefore **Go** could more properly be called execute.

4.4.4 Other options

The other options, find, top, bottom, help, end and Quit, are all standard INGRES options and behave consistently throughout INGRES.

Exercise 4.2

Now you know what to expect, select tables from the qbf startup frame, and select the table chosen in Exercise 4.1, using the cursor. Try out some of the options, but don't try the delete option!

4.5 Using QBF on a Table

Now comes the major part of the book, so make a cup of strong beverage and prepare to be amazed at how easy it all is!

4.5.1 Selecting the operation

Once you have gained Nirvana, all things are possible, so it is with INGRES. Entering the query execution phase with a defined query target you are presented with a frame that looks like Figure 3.

Option selection is simple. Like all the other INGRES frames, press the associated menu key. You can now decide to **append** data, **retrieve** data or **update/delete** data. Help end and quit are the standard INGRES options.

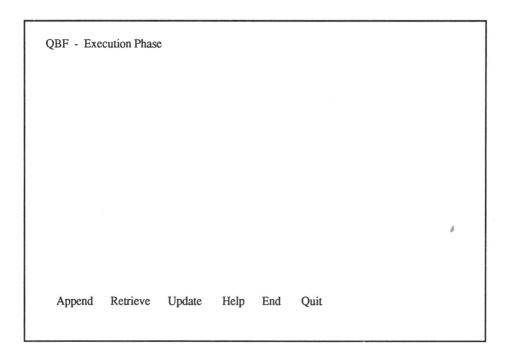

Figure 4.3 Query execution frame

4.5.2 Default forms for QBF

INGRES will create a default form for you to use, this looks something like the form in Figure 4.4.

Some of the form is intelligent guess work by INGRES, and it doesn't look very pretty, however we will be modifying default forms to make them more acceptable in a later chapter.

Exercise 4.3

From now on read the rest of the chapter with the terminal, and try out the techniques you read about. If you have not already done it, select the "Go" option from the tables catalog. Since the next task we are going to look at is appending rows select Append from the execution phase. If you are not sure how to do this, re-read the last section.

DON'T PANIC! Any time you get confused, pressing Exit will eventually take you back to where you started. Any data you add can be deleted, and any table can be recreated. Have fun, it's the best way to learn.

4.5.3 Appending rows

Selection of this option will allow you to add a number of rows to the table. Each frame has a number of fields that can be filled in or left blank.

Simple fields
Each of the fields you see on the default form is a simple field. That is a field that will only display one row's value at a time. This is good for adding a single complex row, like customer details. When your cursor is on the simple field you can move it using the left and right arrow, delete a character using the delete key. If you can't remember, try the sequence HELP, KEYS. You can also re-read the previous chapter.

Entering data is simplicity epitomized. Thank goodness, I hear a voice from the back! Just type in the value you wish to add. If you put more into a field than it will hold the cursor moves on automatically. There is a more efficient way of moving around.

Moving around
To move from field to field use the tab key. This will move you forward through the fields, cycling around, until you decide where to land, like an airliner. If you want to move backwards, it's more tricky. Check with

HELP/KEYS, but normally this function is associated with **Control P** (don't forget to hold the control key down at the same time as pressing the "p" key).

```
┌──────────────────────────────────────────────────────────┐
│                                                          │
│                     EQUIPMENT Table                      │
│                                                          │
│                                                          │
│      Equip Id:                      Equip Desc:          │
│                                                          │
│      Stock Bin:                     No In Stock          │
│                                                          │
│      Reorder Level:                 Price:               │
│                                                          │
│      Location:                      Unit Cost:           │
│                                                          │
│                                                          │
│                                                          │
│      Go    Blank   Order   LastQuery   Help   End        │
│                                                          │
└──────────────────────────────────────────────────────────┘
```

Figure 4.4 Default form for the equipment table

Duplicating previous entries
This is where you get lucky! If you are entering data into simple fields you can avoid extra work (told you you would get lucky) by pressing **Control A**. This will repeat the previously entered data in that field. Don't get too excited though, this doesn't work on table fields.

Saving your row
This is important. If you don't save you will never get rich, and so it goes with databases. After entering the data into the form select **Append** and **QBF** will save the rows after checking them. Any errors that are detected

cause an error message to be displayedand the cursor returned to the place the error occurred or the first field on the form. When you have selected **Append** QBF will send a message to tell you that you have added a row.

Exiting QBF
After you have entered and saved all the rows that you want, use **End** to exit from the QBF form. QBF will then tell you how many rows you have added and return to the previous form.

Exercise 4.4

If you haven't tried appending any rows have a try. If you don't know what to put in, have a look at the test data in Appendix H. This should tell you the type of meaningful data to put into your tables. I know it is hard, to contain your enthusiasm, but don't fill all of the tables at the moment. You will need to keep tables call and call_details for the exercises in the next chapter.

*Make sure that you add the following details to rows in table **operator**.*

> *Operator ID: 23*
> *Operator Name: Walter Winchel*
> *Personnel No: -*
> *Charge Rate: 10*

> *Operator ID: 23*
> *Operator Name: Walter Winchel*
> *Personnel No: -*
> *Charge Rate: 10*

Looks crazy, two operators with identical details? All will be revealed when you get to the section on updating rows!
*Also, if you have time enter all the row details, from Appendix H, in the **equipment** table. This will help in later exercises.*

4.5.4 Retrieving rows

You can easily obtain data, kicking and screaming, from a database table. First you should start from the query execution phase. (If you are lost, press PF3, and press again if needed. Eventually you will return to the known universe, on either the tables catalog, or the query execution phase frame.) Select the **retrieve** option, and the screen changes to the default screen of the table of your choice.

To specify a row that you want extracted from the database table and placed on the screen is simple. Type in an entry in one of the fields on the screen, and select Go to execute. This entry is known as the query specification. If you want to retrieve all the rows then press **Go** without entering any data into the fields.

If no rows are retrieved you may not have typed in the right entry. If one or more rows are retrieved you will have a different menu at the bottom of the screen. Selecting **next** will display the next row in the list. Because of the way that INGRES works you cannot retrieve a previous row (relational theory has no "previous row" concept). Keep pressing **next** until the message "No more rows in query" appears.

If at some time during the display of a set of rows you want to change the query parameters, or make a fresh query, selecting **query** instead of next will cancel the query and place you in the retrieve frame.

Exercise 4.5

*Select **Blank** from the retrieve frame, to blank out all the query specifications, and select Go to retrieve all the rows of the operator table. Try using **Next** to view other rows, stepping through the rows until you get to the end.*

*Retrieve all the rows again, only this time choose **Query** to stop viewing the rows retrieved and to enter another query. Use the **tab** key to move the cursor to the Charge_rt field and enter 10. If you have been following the previous exercises you should, on pressing **Go**, get at least the two rows you appended in Exercise 4.4.*

One of the drawbacks of this method of retrieval is that you must specify the field entry exactly. If you can't remember whether it is John Smith or Steven Smith who has a charge rate of 12, then you could look at all the employees with a charge rate of 12. This is time consuming, but it works. It is not very efficient with large amounts of data though. For this you need to read the next section.

A common lament at Christmas time is "I would like either that car or the larger one, please". In INGRES if you want to specify a range of data you must use a qualification like "either or" in the quote above. The qualification used when you type an exact match is our old friend the equals sign. Other sorts of qualification operators are used.

>   greater than
<   less than
>=   greater than or equal to
<=   less than or equal to
!=   not equal to
or
and

The last two operators should be self explanatory in meaning, although their use needs care. Using these operators is simple; you use them to separate or precede values. The values are typed in to the field on the screen that you want to use to qualify the retrieval. For example, typing the following qualifiers into the Operator ID field on the form has the effects noted alongside.

>24   Match with all rows where the value in this column is greater than 24, but not including 24.

<1.778   Retrieve all the rows with column values that are less than 1.778. This does NOT include matches with 1.778 itself.

Other operators, like **and** and **or**, are used in a different way, but still typed into the appropriate field.

23 and >24   Will retrieve rows with Operator IDs of 23 **and** any rows that have values greater than 24.

23 or 24   Will retrieve rows that have values of 23 or 24 only, no other values.

These operators can be used with character data, but unless you understand the **ascii** character set, which is used to determine the value of a character the results may not be what you expected. To help you retrieve character data if you do not know the exact match, read on!

INGRES goes wild!
If you have an idea about the type of data you want but can't remember exactly which of the Schmidt's details you want to see, why not enter Schmidt into the name field and let the computer do the research. A good idea, but it needs something extra in the way of fairy dust! When you enter only a part of a name the dumb computer thinks that is the whole name, unless you add some **wildcards**. (Poker players can skip the next few sentences). Wildcards are special characters, excluded from use in data, which have the meaning **match any character**. For example:

Sm%   Will retrieve rows where the characters in the column start with Sm and any other characters afterwards. The per cent tells QBF to match any character or number of characters. If you just use the per cent on its own it will retrieve all the rows, as it matches any combinations of characters.

[Ss]%   Will retrieve rows where the first character is either a capital **or** a lower case s. The square brackets here are used to enclose a list of characters, or a range of characters. Any character in the square brackets will replace **one** character only.

J_m   The underscore matches any single character, so this would retrieve Jim, Jem and Jam.

[A-D]27   This little beauty will select all the codes from A27 through to D27. The hyphen specifies a range of characters to be retrieved, not forgetting that any wildcard in square brackets replaces one character.

When you key in these options, with all the wildcards, logical operators, greater than signs, and all the other goodies that you can think of, small fields can be filled with selections. INGRES has already thought about that, however. Simple fields are special in more than one way. They behave more like a window, letting you to put more characters into a field than the field looks as though it will hold. If you have typed a large field you can bring all the characters into view by moving the cursor. Try this with the charge rate in the operator table.

Last Query

Once you have got a complex set of query parameters on the screen and executed, you may want to modify them a little, or re-execute them. Use of the **Last Query** command will re-display the last query parameters and allow you to edit them if you want.

Viewing the rows

Building the qualifications is only part of a query. After you have qualified a query you can execute it by pressing **Go. Go** reads the qualifications and formats them so that the system understands them, and the database management system retrieves the row(s) that are specified. This can result in the retrieval of multiple rows. The data used in Exercise 4.4 will produce two rows. I know that they are identical, but that is for later use.

A small digression. INGRES stores data in operating system files, which have different storage structures, used for different types of retrievals. The important thing here is that INGRES will allow you to enter duplicate rows in some of the storage structures. The default structure, the one you get automatically, is a heap structure, where rows are piled indiscriminately on top of each other, no checking for duplicates, no fast retrieval. This is the default because, if you think about it, the first job after creating a table is to fill it with data, and this is the best structure for bulk data loading.

Back to the subject in mind. When rows are retrieved, a new menu of choices are displayed on the menu line. The options are **Next, Query, Help** and **End**. Help and End are the usual INGRES options, but **Next** will retrieve and display the next row in the dataset (that's what a group of retrieved rows is called). Each row in the dataset is displayed until the last row. Pressing **Next** will cause a message "No more rows" to be displayed, the fields blanked out, and a new menu to be displayed on the menu line.   If you have a retrieved a large number of rows, but you have decided to change the query qualifications, returning to the query menu line is easy. Just press **Query** and your current group of rows is terminated as if there were no more rows.

EQUIPMENT Table						
Equip Id:	Equip Desc:	Stock Bin:	No In Stock	Reorder Level:	Price:	Loca
7774	Ream 120g Paper	22	100	50	15.00	W2
7771	Ream 80g Paper	21	250	100	12.00	W2
7761	Executive Chair	9	2	1	241.00	W1
7760	Mahog 2dr Desk	10	2	1	340.00	W1

Go   Blank   Order   LastQuery   Help   End

Figure 4.5 Equipment form showing data in descending order

Sorting the output

Requesting output from a database table can give you a headache, especially if you are not sure where in the dataset your chosen row comes. To solve this you can request a different sort order from the way in which data is stored in the table. This is especially useful for displaying all the rows in a dataset in ascending order of salary. In our sample database the equipment table has a **price** column. It may be handy to display all the rows for stock in location "Small Warehouse" in

descending order of price.

First enter "Small Warehouse" in the location column and then select **Order**. This will give you the **QBF** frame with a slightly different format. The cursor is moved about the screen as normal, and you sort a column by putting the cursor on that column and entering a number.

The number entered, between 1 and 127, is the number of that field in the sort order. Putting a "1" in the field makes it the primary sorting field. Other fields can be ordered, by using the other numbers allowed. To sort a field in descending order follow the sort priority number with a "d" or a "D". The equipment table would look like Figure 4.5. Another point to note about Figure 4.5 is the format of the display. This is typical of a display that is wider, by default, than the screen can hold. To view the parts of the screen that are hidden use the left arrow of the keyboard, or some other nominated key. Don't forget the **Help** menu item if you need help on the action of keys.

Exercise 4.6

Try retrieving rows from a table of your choice. Amazing the difference if you choose a table that has rows in though! Follow some of the guidelines below to make sure you try out all the different combinations of retrieval:

- Retrieve all the rows in the operator table.

- Retrieve all the rows in the operator table where the operator id is greater than 23.

- Retrieve all the rows in the operator table with operator names sorted in ascending order.

Try some other retrievals, and note the duplicate rows in the operator table

4.5.5 Updating rows

When you have inserted rows into a table, it is not uncommon to have to change some details, after all we have put duplicate rows into the database in Exercise 4.4. To update rows, you first have to find them, then change them. On selection of **update** from the query execution phase frame, a default form is displayed and the menu line has the following options:

Go   Executes the query

Blank   Clears the current entries from the frame

LastQuery Displays the last query specification for editing

Order   Sets the order of rows for sorting

All the other options are normal INGRES options. The **update** frame is also where rows are deleted.

Retrieving rows for update
As previously mentioned rows must be retrieved before they can be updated or deleted. The query qualification is produced using the rules and techniques in the **Retrieve** section. Once a query has been qualified, pressing **Go** will select the dataset for your operations.

Changing data
Moving around the update frame, after retrieving rows, is done by **tab** and **Control P**. Don't use the return key to move, as you will lose the data on the field you move from. When the cursor is on a field that you want to change use the **Insert** and **Delete** keys to change the data. Can't remember which keys those are? What have you got a **Help** key for?

Deleting data
To delete a row from a database table take the **Delete** option from the **Update** frame. The **Delete** option is used to erase an entire row of data. All the rows in a dataset that are deleted are saved in a temporary store, and the changes are not sent to the database until **Save** is selected from the update menu.

Saving your work
Once you have changed data it does not mean that the data in the database is changed, as the changes have not been passed to the database. Selecting

Save will pass the data to the database. If you don't want to save the changes, after trying out the update option **End** will let you exit. **End** is very well mannered though; it will ask if you really want to exit without saving changes.

Exercise 4.7

Remember the crazy row values you put in in Exercise 4.4? This is where you put them right. The values should be

Operator ID:	*24*
Operator Name:	*Samuel Wong*
Personnel No:	*HL241*
Charge Rate:	*10*

Operator ID:	*28*
Operator Name:	*Dan Rather*
Personnel No:	*HL1223*
Charge Rate:	*10*

This is about the stage that people usually say " What does this thing allow me to input mad, bad values for?" Well the answer is "Read more of the book, try not to sleep, as the chapter on Vifred will help solve this problem".

4.6 Chapter Review

In this chapter you have covered the following topics.

o   Starting QBF on your database.

o   Selecting single tables and using QBF with them.

o   Adding rows to tables using the **Append** option.

o   Selecting one or more rows using the **Retrieve** option.

o   Changing the contents of rows using the **Update** option.

o   Deleting rows using the **Update** option.

4.7 Quick Reference

Getting into QBF

   Select **Queries** from INGRES menu

or
```
qbf <databasename>
```

Working on tables

Select **Tables** from the QBF menu

Retrieving

   Select **Retrieve** from the QBF Execution Frame.

   Move the cursor to the field you wish to select on and type in your
   selection criteria (see section 4.5.4 if you can't remember). Take
   the **Go** option to execute your query.

   To select all the rows in a table take the **Go** option without any
   selection criteria in the fields.

Updating

   Select **Update** from the QBF Execution Frame.

   Select the row or rows to be changed by using the same techniques
   outlined in Retrieving, above.

   Move the cursor to the value that you want to change, and make the
   change.

Make the change permanent by selecting **Save** from the menu.

Deleting

Select **Update** from the QBF Execution Frame.

Select the row or rows to be deleted by using the same techniques outlined in Retrieving, above.

Select **Delete** and when INGRES has deleted the row or rows select the **Save** option to make the change permanent.

Appending

Select **Append** from the QBF Execution Frame.

Move the cursor to the field you wish to enter data into and key in the data.

Select **Append** to commit the row to the database.

Chapter 5

Complex Data Manipulation

5.1 Introduction

In this chapter the differences in technique between simple and table field data retrievals are explained with examples. The concept of multiple table retrieval is introduced, and **JoinDef**s are described. Master and detail relationships are reviewed, referring to previous chapters. **JoinDef**s are explained with emphasis on joins, rules and displays referring back to previous chapters. A join between two sample tables is defined and saved, followed by an examination of the **JoinDef**s catalog.

     Well, there you are, ploughed through the book so far, and what have you got? Lot's of information about databases, tables and rows. I still have not told you how to get at tables that are related by joined columns? Before we go there a little more on joins.

5.1.1 Joining tables

From previous chapters we have seen that tables hold related information. Sometimes that information is held in more than one table, and the tables are related or linked by some commonality of data, the join fields. These tables can be linked by defining the **join definition**. This is shortened to **JoinDef** in INGRES.

     To define a join INGRES needs to know what tables are linked, and what columns contain the common values. Joins are illustrated in Figure 5.1.

5.1.2 Types of joins

You are allowed two types of joins in QBF, master to master, and master to detail. Master to master joins are relational equi-joins, one to one joins. Master to detail joins are one to many joins. The decision on the type of join used would be made at system design time. In our sample system a one to many example is demonstrated by the joining of call to call_details.

Joins can be also be chained together to give even more complex retrieval as in Figure 5.2

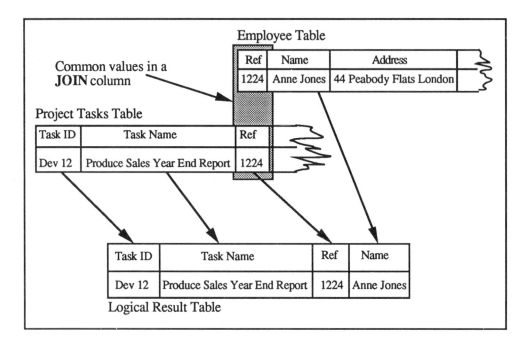

Figure 5.1 Two table join

If you are at all unsure of joins, re-read the relevant parts in Chapter 1 on database concepts, and possibly spend some time with the table definitions and design exercises in Chapter 2. After that try Exercise 5.1, below.

Exercise 5.1

Select tables to join from the designs you made in Chapter 2, or use the tables call and call_details from the table definitions used in Chapter 3. Decide which of the tables will be a master, and which of the tables will be the detail.

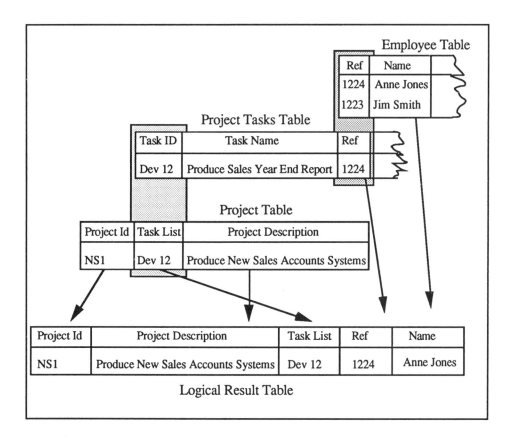

Figure 5.2 A cascade of joins

5.2 Creating a Join Definition

5.2.1 Getting there - How to start JoinDefs

Starting **JoinDefs** is easy from INGRES menu, just select **JoinDefs** and there you are. Starting from the operating system is almost as easy. All you need to do is to type

```
qbf <database name> -j
```

Both of these methods give get you to the **JoinDefs** catalog frame, as shown in Figure 5.3.

```
 ┌──────────────────────────────────────────────────────────────────┐
 │  QBF -  JoinDefs Catalog                                          │
 │                                                                    │
 │   ┌──────────────┬────────────┬───────────────────────────────┐   │
 │   │  Name        │  Owner     │  Short Remark                  │   │
 │   │              │            │                                │   │
 │   │  call_in     │  petem     │  call and call_details for call reception │
 │   │  call_actions│  petem     │  call_details and action for reporting on actions │
 │   │              │            │                                │   │
 │   │              │            │                                │   │
 │   │              │            │                                │   │
 │   │              │            │                                │   │
 │   └──────────────┴────────────┴───────────────────────────────┘   │
 │                                                                    │
 │       Place cursor on row and select desired operation from menu   │
 │  Create  Destroy  Edit  Rename  MoreInfo  Go  Find  Top  Bottom  Help  End  Quit  > │
 └──────────────────────────────────────────────────────────────────┘
```

Figure 5.3 JoinDefs catalog frame

Exercise 5.2

Keep the notes of decisions from Exercise 5.1, you will need them later. Start qbf on your test database, and select joindef from the qbf menu.

5.2.2 What you can see

The frame displayed with frightening speed when **JoinDef**s is selected is the **JoinDef**s catalog frame. The catalog table field may be empty, or at least it should be, as we have yet to create a **JoinDef**. If the catalog is not empty, suspect someone, it may even be you, of jumping the gun! There are a number of options, which we will examine later, but for now we will look at the create option, after all you need to create a **JoinDef** to play with.

Exercise 5.3

*Select create from the **JoinDef** catalog frame, even though there are no names in the catalog.*

5.2.3 Getting down to join definitions

In this next section a series of explanations and exercises step you through creating and using a **JoinDef**. This section is best read in one or two chunks, sitting at a terminal and doing the exercises as they occur. If you want to rest, the best place to do it is straight after the append exercises.

Naming a JoinDef
JoinDefs all need a name. Naming conventions are the same for tables, and I haven't time to type them in again. Check Chapters 2 and 3 on design. One thing, however, meaningful (what a great word!) names should rule, OK? If you are using the example and joining **call** and **call_details** together names like "call_join" or "call_det_j" are typical. It is sometimes helpful to put a **_j** at the end of the **JoinDef** name, to signify a join rather than a table name.

Exercise 5.4

*The cursor should be placed on the **JoinDef** name field, and type in a name for your **JoinDef** (call_in_j would describe the **JoinDef** neatly).*

Master and detail tables

Once a **JoinDef** is named the next step is to name the tables that you chose in Exercise 5.1. For the sake of simplicity we will look at a master to detail or one to many join. The **role** column is used to indicate that the table in that row is either a master(m) or a detail(d) table.

Hint: Moving around any INGRES frame is always the same, tab moves from field to field without affecting the contents and return will delete the column from the cursor position and move onto the next field.

Exercise 5.5

Enter the names of your master table and detail table in the appropriate place. Don't forget to use tab to move onto the next field that you want.

Abbreviations and what they can do

Now you have got a master and detail table named, you will have noticed the optional abbreviation column. Abbreviations are shortened forms of the table names. They are mostly used in complex joins of many tables, to simplify a **JoinDef**, and always used when you join a table to itself.

Table fields or not table fields?

Before going further there is only one field to complete. This is where you decide on a table field format for the detail rows displayed or use simple fields. When choosing a table field or not, remember that in a master to master join **ALL** the rows in a **JoinDef** will be in the chosen format. In a master to detail join only the rows in the detail table are formated, the fields in the master table are always displayed as simple fields. For now we want to display as many rows of detail as possible, but you can experiment with this option afterwards.

5.2.4 Using the new definition

Starting and where it gets you

Now you have a complete join definition, as shown in Figure 5.4, it's time to test out the way in which it behaves. Do this before you save the **JoinDef**, and you save a lot of editing. Selecting **Go** from the menu line will take you from the **JoinDef** definition frame into the **QBF** execution frame, from where you will select one of the options to manipulate data. Attempt Exercise 5.6 before continuing.

Exercise 5.6

*Select go from the **JoinDef** Definition frame, leaving the table field format option as "y". You will be presented with another frame, an old friend by now, the QBF execution frame. Before carrying on with the chapter select the **Append** option.*

If the exercises have been followed, there should have been no problem in selecting **Go** and **Append**, and having the default form displayed. If you are following a different table and join structure, and have problems, first look at the names of the columns in the tables joined.

Default forms

When you have selected the **Append, Retrieve**, or **Update** options you are given a data entry form. This form contains fields, and columns in a table field which correspond to the columns in the tables selected in the **JoinDef** definition frame. This form may not look very attractive, and the fields/columns may not be very thoughtfully placed. The form can be modified in appearance and functionality later. All the default form does is to allow you to test out the **JoinDef**. Each of the tables named in the **JoinDef** has a section on the form headed by the table name.

Moving around

Moving in the default form follows the normal INGRES behaviour for your installation, **Tab** move from field to field, and column to column in table fields. If you are still not sure, check with your manual, or system manager.

QBF - JoinDef Definition Frame

    JoinDef Name: call_in

    For each table in the JoinDef, enter table name (with optional
    abbreviation for table name) below. For Master/Detail JoinDefs
    enter Master or Detail under Role. (Default is Master if blank.)

Role	Table Name	Abbreviation
m	call	call
d	call_details	call_details

    Table Field Format? (y/n): YES

  Select the "Go" menu item to run the JoinDefinition.

  Go Blank ChangeDisplay Joins Rules Save Help End Quit

Figure 5.4 Completed **JoinDef** frame

Join-columns

One point to notice, join-columns are highlighted, and there is only one
field for a join-column. A join-column in a detail table, in table field
format, is not displayed, but the identical column name displayed for the
master table is highlighted. Figure 5.5 shows a join between **call** and
call_details. The common column is **customer_no**. You can see that
although customer_no is part of call_details it only appears under call, as
there may be many rows retrieved for each row in call.

    INGRES will create a default join based on identical join-column
names. If the join-columns don't have the same name, then INGRES won't
allow you to test your join, until you have defined your join. Read
further, and read the exercises as well to find out how to define joins.

Adding data

When we look at adding data to a **JoinDef** we will work with master/detail joins, master to master joins can be treated as an ordinary QBF data entry form.

Adding data to a **JoinDef** is like adding data to any other data entry form, except for table field entries. Data is entered into columns in the table field, using INGRES standard commands. Adding more rows to a table field than it will hold is no problem as the field will scroll up more empty rows as you need them. When enough data has been entered, you can enter more than one row in a table field, select **Append** to add the master and detail rows. You will see a reply from INGRES on the bottom of the screen, telling you the number of master and detail rows appended.

If you want to add a row in between other table field rows, place the cursor where you want the new row to be and select **Insert**. This is not needed if you are entering a number of rows in a blank table field. Exercise 5.5 will give you some practice in appending rows.

CALL Table

Customer No: Call Id:

Operator Id: Start Time:

End Time:

CALL_DETAILS TABLE(S):

Equip_id	Description	Action

Go   Blank   LastQuery   Order   Help   End

Figure 5.5 Default frame for join exercise

Leaving quietly

When you have finished filling the database with all the important information, you need to exit from your session. Taking the **End** option will take you back to the **QBF** execution frame. If you haven't **Append**ed the data on the current display, INGRES will tell you and ask if you still want to exit. Answering **no** will allow you to take the **Append** option and save those rows.

Exercise 5.7

You should be sitting in front of a screen showing the default for your **JoinDef**. *It is important that you have selected the* **Append** *option at the QBF execution frame, as this exercise is about adding rows to a joindef.*

Enter some call details. If you haven't got any data to work with, use the details below. You are going to input details of a number of telephone calls. The call details will be used later by despatch and other staff and their actions recorded. Don't worry about making mistakes with the data, as you can always delete it and start again.

Call Id	*23*	*Customer No*	*273*
Operat_id	*55*	*Start Time*	*now*
End Time	*now*		

Equip ID	*7780*
Descrip	*Two hole punch broken, still under warranty*

Equip ID	*7781*
Descrip	*Leather blotter needed*

Call Id	*26*	*Customer No*	*472*
Operat_id	*55*	*Start Time*	*now*
End Time	*now*		

Equip ID	*7760*
Descrip	*Re-equiping new office, new desk*

Equip ID	*7761*
Descrip	*Re-equiping new office, chair*

Eguip ID	*7780*
Descrip	*Re-equiping new office, two hole punch*

Don't forget to select **Append** *after you have entered each set of master/detail rows. When you have finished select* **END** *to return to the QBF execution phase frame menu*

Retrieving data
Data that is entered can be retrieved by entering qualifications in either the simple fields or the columns of the table field. INGRES takes care of the synchronization between the join columns. Wildcards are allowed, INGRES behaves consistently for retrievals. Exercise 5.8 will help you become more familiar with retrievals.

Exercise 5.8

You should still have the QBF execution phase frame on the screen, if not, select **Go** *from the* **JoinDef** *menu. Try some retrievals. If you have been following these exercises try out these retrievals.*

1. *Retrieve all masters, and use* **NextMaster** *to view the detail rows for these masters. Some of the masters displayed may not have any detail rows. You can add some later if you want to.*

2. *Retrieve all the call details between* **call_id** *20 and 30.*

3. *Retrieve all the calls received for* **equip_id** *7780.*

4. *Retrieve all the calls with "punch" in the description part of the table field.*

*Use **Next_Master** to view more master rows. When you have finished, select **End** to return to the QBF execution phase frame.*

Updating data

Updates in **JoinDef**s are carried out in much the same way as in table-based QBF. First find the row or rows you want to update, then update them. When viewing an update frame on a **JoinDef** some new options will be displayed.

> **NextMaster** Displays the next row of data from master and the associated detail table fields.
>
> **NxtDetail** Displays the next row of detail in an equi-join.
>
> **AddDetail** Adds a new detail row to the currently displayed master.
>
> **Delete** Deletes data, see section on deleting rows

As you can see from the list of options, a lot depends on the format of the frame. However there are parts of the form that should not be updated. Restrictions can be placed on the fields and columns updated by using **Rules**, see below. Next try Exercise 5.9.

Exercise 5.9

*You should still have the QBF execution phase frame on the screen, if not, select **Go** from the joindef menu. Select **Update** from the execution phase menu. Try these updates on the data you have entered from the exercises. Don't forget to select **Save** to send your changed data to the database.*

> *1.   Update **call_id** 23 and change the equipment id 7781 to 7784, changing the corresponding description to 12 inch ruler.*
>
> *2.   Update the start and end time on **call_id** 26 to the current*

---

time using the date word "now"

3.   *Delete a detail row from **call_id** 26 by using the*
        ***DetailRow** option, after chosing **delete** from the JoinDef*
        execution frame.

Don't update the join column yet, that comes into another exercise. Select
***End** after you have finished, and also **End** from the **QBF** execution*
frame. This should return you to the JoinDef definition frame.

Deleting rows
When the **Delete** option is taken from the **Update** frame a new menu is
displayed. The options on this new menu will be shown on **JoinDefs** and
QBF frames that have table fields.

Master   Deletes the master record currently
                        displayed, and **ALL** its detail records. Watch
                        out for this one, it destroys everything for
                        that master. This is useful in our example
                        databases, to delete calls that are no longer
                        current.

AllDetailRows   This command deletes all the detail rows for
                        the current master row. Don't forget that a
                        table field is a window onto a dataset, and
                        will delete the hidden rows as well as the
                        visible rows.

DetailRow   Deletes the single detail row indicated by the
                        cursor in the table field display.

Detail   This will delete the currently displayed detail
                        row on a form with no table field display.

AllRows   Deletes all the rows in the table field, visible
                        and invisible. This option is normally used
                        when a master/master join uses a table field
                        format.

*Saving your **JoinDef***

When you are completely satisfied with your **JoinDef** it is time to save it. If you exit from the **JoinDef** definition frame without selecting the **Save** option, you will lose the work you have done creating a **JoinDef**. Leaving the definition frame causes the **JoinDef** catalogs frame to be displayed, and the **JoinDef** created will now be displayed in the catalog table field.

Exercise 5.10

*Save your JoinDef, by choosing the **Save** option from the JoinDef definition frame. You should see the name of your join definition in the JoinDef catalog frame, when the definition has been saved. Don't leave the JoinDef catalog frame, as you have more work to do!*

5.3 Tricks of the Joiner's Art

The basics of using **JoinDefs** are simple, but the scope of the simple **JoinDef** can be enhanced by using a few other options. These are not necessarily extras, in the case of the join definitions, some **JoinDefs** will give inconsistent results if joins are not accurately declared.

5.3.1 Specifying join columns

Declaring non default joins

INGRES is normally good at guessing how tables are joined together, but only when the join columns have the same name! If you are joining tables on more than one column you will also need to declare the extra joins. This is where the abbreviations come in helpful.

Modifications to the joins are made in the **JoinDef** join specification frame. Using the **Joins** option from the **JoinDef** definition frame you are transported, on a balmy breeze, to the specifications form. Decide on the columns that you are going to join, using the **GetTableDef** option to help you. This is covered after Exercise 5.12. Move the cursor to one of the columns in the first table field and enter the table name, a dot and the join column name. Enter the table.column name for the second part of the join. Do this for each table.column name combination that you need to reflect accurately the way to join tables.

```
QBF - JoinDef JoinSpecification
```

Column	Join	Column
c.call_id	MD	d.call_id
c.call_id	MM	a.call_id

To get help on a table, enter the table name or identifier
below and select the "Get TableDef" menu item.

Table (or Abbreviation) : call_details

Column	Data Type
call_id	integer
equip_id	integer
description	varchar(100)
action	varchar(100)

Rules   GetTableDef   Forget   Help   End

Figure 5.6 Three table **JoinDef**

Try Exercise 5.11, but don't forget that **One** master table must join to **One** detail table, and **One** detail table should join to **One** detail table. If you are unsure about this, look at the cascade of joins in Figure 5.2. and the example in Figure 5.6. In Figure 5.6 you notice that a table, abbreviated to "c" is joined to a table abbreviated to "d". The next part of the join is to link table "c" to table "a". Thus you have a master to master join, making them joint masters. This is preceded by joining one of the masters to a detail table to complete the three table join. It is worth experimenting with this to gain a full understanding.

Exercise 5.11

*Go from the JoinDef catalog frame by selecting the **edit** option with the cursor on the JoinDef you have defined and saved in the preceding exercises. From the JoinDef definition frame select **ChangeDisplay** to make some changes to the fields or columns displayed. Remove **custno** from the master and **equip_id** from the detail table. Take the **end** option from JoinDef Change Display form. Try out your new JoinDef by selecting **Go** from the JoinDef definition frame.*

Rules

The **Rules** option can be used from both the join definition and specification forms. Modifications to the rules affect the way in which rows can be deleted or updated. Let us look at the update rules first.

Update rules can be changed by using **tab** to move to the table/column combination, and entering **Yes** or **No**. In the **Update?** column a **yes** means that a change to the field on the form will be sent to that database table; a **no** means that although you can make changes to the screen, they won't be sent to the database. Update rules only work on join columns, as they are the only ones shown in the update table field on the rules form.

Delete rules affect the whole row or rows for the table named in the delete table field. The valid entries are **Yes** and **No**. A **yes** entered against a table name means rows in that table can be deleted by normal QBF delete commands. Guess what? A **no** means rows can't be deleted.

These rules are normally used as the first level of control for the user. If you want people to change call details, for example, without affecting the call table, entering **Yes** against the call_details table and **No** against the call table would have that effect.

Exercise 5.12

*From the JoinDef definition frame select **Rules** and experiment with the effects of saying **yes** to update call_details, and updating a join field. If you change **call_id** 23, what is the result to the master table and the detail table?*

*Try changing the delete rules for the **call** table to **No** and select **Master** from the delete menu.*

*The easiest way to check on the results is to back out of JoinDefs and check the table contents by using the **tables** option from QBF startup frame (Chapter 4).*

GetTableDef

Can't remember the columns in your table, and the paper with your notes is in the bin? INGRES has the solution, **GetTableDef**. Use tab to place the cursor at the **Table (or Abreviation)** prompt. Enter your table name and select **GetTableDef**, and the table definition will unfold before your eyes.

Changing the display of **JoinDefs**

Not all columns for a table may need displaying; this is especially true of management reporting functions. Generally management reporting is not concerned with minute details but with a broader picture. The appearance of forms can be changed dramatically by using the **Vifred** visual forms editor, discussed in the next two chapters. Simple, fast changes can be made to **JoinDefs** by using the **ChangeDisplay** facility offered from the **JoinDef** definition form. This can help the form's appearance by letting you delete columns from the default form.

The **JoinDef** change display form gives you a list of columns for each table in the **JoinDef**. **NextTable** shows each table's details in turn. Moving the cursor to a column name in the table field, and selecting **Delete** removes that column from the default form display. Try out these changes on a JoinDef. The one in Exercise 5.13 is a good idea.

Exercise 5.13

*From the **JoinDef** definition frame add a new table to your existing **JoinDef**; **action** seems good, labelling it with the role **detail**. Before trying this **JoinDef** out add a new join by selecting **Joins** from the **JoinDef** definition frame. You will need to check that the detail tables are joined together, and the master table is joined to one of the detail tables. (Don't forget to use **GetTableDef** to check on column names.)*

*Once you have specified your join use **End** to return to the **JoinDef** definition frame, and the **Go** option from there to test out the new join.*

Forget and Undo

Like Batman and Robin, the dynamic duo of **Forget** and **Undo** will save the day if you are not happy with the changes you have made. They are shown on various **JoinDef** frames, and always have the effect of cancelling changes back to the last save, or the default for new **JoinDef**s. After selecting **Forget** or **Undo** INGRES will return control to the previous frame.

5.3.2 Operations at the JoinDef catalog frame

These are options available from the **JoinDef** catalog frame. They are dealt with fully in the INGRES manuals.

Create

This option will allow you to create (what a surprise?) a **JoinDef**. Selecting this option will give you a blank **JoinDef** frame, ready for naming.

Destroy

This is the one that undoes all that experimentation and work. Selecting this option will delete the entry the cursor is on in the **JoinDefs** catalog. Don't despair or worry about taking this option by accident, INGRES is well mannered enough to ask if you really want to delete your **JoinDef**.

Edit

Remember that **JoinDef** you created as an example? Use of this option will let you edit the **JoinDef**, even changing the name and saving it as a new version. When you use this option, making changes to the **JoinDef**, don't forget to save the changes.

Rename

You'll never guess what this option does? Yes, it renames the **JoinDef**. This cannot be used to create new **JoinDefs**; for that use **edit**.

Go

The **GO** option lets you execute the **JoinDef** of your choice. This takes you into the **QBF** execution phase frame, from where you can choose to **Append**, **Retrieve**, **Update**, etc.

MoreInfoFind

After you have selected to **Save** your **JoinDef** you are presented with a screen that shows both the short remark and long remark about the object you are saving. Short remarks are a brief identifier that gives extra help about the object, expanding the name into something meaningful. The long remark however is only displayed again when the **MoreInfoFind** option is selected. Wouldn't it be great if the long remark held information on the purpose of the **JoinDef**, its author, and where it fits into the whole system? This would not only be good if this system were to be used by others, but when your inevitable promotion to Company President arrives, someone else may have to take responsibility for the system. Just think how they will love and respect you, even in the morning.

Top, Bottom, Help, End, Quit

Well, these are old familiar commands by now. If you don't know what they are, you should read the previous chapters. I'll give you a hint though, they are all standard INGRES forms commands.

5.4 Chapter Review

In this chapter you have covered the following topics:

o   The differences between simple and table fields

o   Master and detail relationships

o   Naming tables to join

o   Retrieving, updating, appending, and deleting data using a JoinDef

o   Saving your JoinDef

o   Three or more table joins

o   Changing JoinDef displays

o   Changing delete and update rules

o   Using options from the JoinDef catalogs

5.5 Quick Reference

Creating a JoinDef

-   Select **JoinDef** from the QBF startup frame

-   Select **Create** from the **JoinDef** catalog frame

-   Enter **Table** names

-   Enter **Role** (Master or Detail) of the table in the join

    Master is the default if the Role is left blank

-   Decide on the use of table fields and change the form accordingly

-   Use **Go** to test the JoinDef

-   **Save** the JoinDef if it is correct

Modify rules

-   Select **Rules** from the JoinDef definition or specification frame

-   **Tab** to **Update** rules field and enter **Yes** or **No**

-   **Tab** to **Delete** rules field and and enter **Yes** or **No**

-   Select **Forget** to return the form to its original state

- Select **End** to complete your changes to Rules

Adding a join

- Add a Table name and Role to the JoinDef definition frame

- Select **Joins** from the JoinDef definition frame

- Enter the abbreviation and column name of the new table

- **Tab** to the next column and enter another table and column name for the column which will contain the common values for the join

- Select **End** to complete editing the rules

- Select **Go** to test the join

Modify appearance

- Select **ChangeDisplay** from the JoinDef definition frame

- **Delete** any columns from the first table displayed

- Use **NextTable** to edit the display on the next table on the screen

- Select **Undo** if you have deleted too many columns

- Select **End** to complete the change of display

- Select **Go** to test your changes

Chapter 6

Improving the Looks

"All that glisters is not gold, but a good looking screen helps a lot."

6.1 What is this thing called "vifred"

Uptil now we have been looking at default forms, and very default they are too. Default forms are OK for "quick and dirty" functionality, giving you a boost by being easy to use, but not very pretty. Just think of all the poor data entry people who will have to work with your screens. This is where you benefit mankind with attractive easy-to-read screens, using display colours, lines, boxes, etc.

Now is the time to start editing default forms and creating blank forms using the INGRES tool, Vifred. What a great name. "Vifred", grace, style, elegance? Well the truth is not far from that. Vifred is a contraction of VIsual FoRms EDitor. In this chapter you will learn to make your forms look more attractive and easy to use. You will find out how easy it is to move items about the screen, and prevent the input of wrong or illegal values.

6.1.1 Editing default forms

Vifred is a productivity tool, like most **INGRES** tools and default forms can be edited by **QBF**. In fact **Vifred** uses the same method to create default forms as **QBF** used to display them. Once a default form is created it can be edited, names changed, underlined, flashed, boxed and all sorts. After a default form has been changed, it can be saved, and used by **QBF** later on. **JoinDef** default forms can also be used for editing and saving. This is the fastest way of creating forms for use in **INGRES**.

100

6.1.2 Blank forms

Blank forms are used in **INGRES** to create new forms, popup forms, discussed below, and more usually menu forms for use in the 4GL. A blank form can be created, by selecting - you guessed it - BlankForm, from the **Vifred** menu frame in Figure 6.1. This chapter will not show you how to create a form from a blank screen, as this is a straightforward task, especially if you read the INGRES Forms and Menus and Report Writer manual. After this chapter you may want to try out the **BlankForm** option, as you will use this in Chapter 9 when you are defining frames for reports and forms.

6.1.3 Lots of goodies

Vifred lets you produce some sophisticated screen displays. Those attributes, flashing, inverse video, etc. that can be allocated during a **Vifred** session will be outlined in this chapter, however one of the most useful and important functions that **Vifred** can give is the ability to create a pop-up "window". This is a Frame (a 4GL term for a screen form and program code combination. Remember this from Chapter 3?) and is used under the control of **ABF**. This facility is outside the scope of the book so you will have to wait for "Son of User Guide - The Sequel".

6.2 Forms

The purpose of a database management system is to manage data that is input, and display forms with results, and reports. This leads to the conclusion that display forms for input and output make up an important part of INGRES. Before we take a look at **Vifred**, we need to understand a few terms and definitions.

6.2.1 Trim

Trim describes decorative or informative objects on the screen, a form heading, a box, underlining, instructions, etc. Trim does not have any attributes, other than those that can be set by the form editor.

6.2.2 Fields

A field is made up of three parts, firstly, the **title**, which usually reflects the type of data displayed by the field, such as "Sales Order:" or "Account Number:".

The next part of the field is the **data window**, starting with a character signifying the data type of the window. This is followed by a number of underscores signifying the number of characters or digits in the field. This is only to give an idea of how the data is represented on screen. We will look at data formats and attributes in more detail later on.

The final part of a field is the **data attributes**, which can be separated into two further types, display attributes and form attributes.

I know that I said three parts, but in fact there is a fourth part, the underlying storage element. This is used in 4GL programming, so I will not be dealing with this any further.

Display attributes
Many display attributes can be set, like inverse video, to alter the display of the screen. Some, like **upper case**, affect data during input. All of these are arbitrarily grouped as display attributes, so that I can talk about them in this chapter.

Form attributes
Form data attributes help the user and the developer by setting some conditions for the use of the field. These are typically for checking input values, say salary must be between 10,000 and 20,000 monetary units. Or making sure that a customer number is already on file. These attributes and their use is discussed in a later chapter.

6.3 Crank the Engine

6.3.1 Starting up

Well, here we are again, glad I used a wordprocessor on this. This is where I introduce you to some old friends.

From the command line prompt use `vifred <dbname>` to start

vifred. You can add some command line flags to start up on specific tables etc., but for the moment we would like a start on a catalog table field. The ability that INGRES has to produce catalogs as a picking list is always helpful. You can get at vifred and the forms catalog from INGRES menu, but I am not going to tell you how. You should be able to work it out for yourselves. Whichever way you choose will display the catalogs frame like the one shown in Figure 6.1. Have a look at Exercise 6.1 and then carry on with the rest of the chapter.

```
VIFRED - Forms Catalog

 _____
| Name              | Owner | Short Remark                  |
|_____|_____|_____|
| customer          | petem | Customer based on table default|
| call_in           | petem | Call_in, based on joindefault |
|                   |       |                               |
|                   |       |                               |
|                   |       |                               |
|                   |       |                               |
|                   |       |                               |
|_____|_____|_____|

        Place cursor on row and select desired operation from menu.
  Create   Destroy   Edit   Rename   MoreInfo   >  :
```

Figure 6.1 Vifred forms catalog

Exercise 6.1

Start Vifred from either the operating system level or from INGRES

Menu. You should see your screen display a catalog of vifred forms, although there aren't any, as you haven't created any yet.

Once you have the catalogs on the screen the menu options are available. Before continuing from here, remember that some of these selections are the same for each INGRES utility that you use, and if you are in doubt try **Help***. Since we are going to start with a fresh form, and there may not be any entries in the catalog, selecting* **Create** *will give you another menu line. It is possible to create a form from a blank screen but for the moment we will deal with editing an existing form or default.*

6.3.2 Default forms

This is where you specify the easy part. The default forms allow you to be presented, after due pomp and ceremony, with a form for you to edit that already contains most of the features you want. This form has been created from the system catalogs, in the same way that **QBF** creates forms. The only difference in these forms is that you can edit them and save the edits.

Hint: Remember that all the INGRES subsystems like **QBF** and **Vifred** use similar keys and menus to perform similar functions.

Table default
Table default is the menu option for creating a form from the table structure. Vifred reads the table specification and arranges fields on the form according to the table definitions. This will only put fields on the form that are in the table definition. For additional fields from other tables combined, use the **JoinDefault** option.

JoinDefault
After the hard work in defining your joins in earlier chapters you can select the **JoinDefault** option and INGRES will draw a default form according to the join specification previously saved.

Blank form
A form can be created from a blank form, creating trim and fields as needed. This is also the method for creating a trim only form as a menu

screen. There will not be any opportunity during the exercises, but INGRES Forms and Menus and Report Writer manual contains further information.

Exercise 6.2

*Take the **create** option from the **Vifred** forms catalogs if you haven't already done so, to create a form, and select **tabledefault** from the next menu shown. As the rest of the exercises are based on the **customer** table, enter **customer** in response to the prompt. Try and restrain your enthusiasm and do not jump the gun and carry on. Return to the text and the next exercise will come fast enough.*

6.3.3 Field formats for forms

As you look at a form like Figure 6.2 showing simple fields (remember those?) you will see the fields laid out on the form. Each field has a title, like cust_no. The title is the same as the column name from the table description, but has an uppercase first character. This is followed by a "c" or an "f". The f or c indicates the format of the data that you are going to display or key in to this field. More details can be discovered about data formats later in the chapter.

Exercise 6.3

*Now is the time finally to see what form you are going to edit. If you haven't passed this point, choose **Simple fields** from the menu and watch the default form appear on the screen. You will notice that instead of the blank fields on a **QBF** default form, each of the fields on a **Vifred** default form has something in them. Carry on with the chapter now, leaving all the interesting stuff for the next exercise.*

6.3.4 Vifred menu

Well, there are some old friends in the **Vifred** menu. Help and quit will behave as they do on all the other **INGRES** menus, **Create** and **Edit** bring up submenus which allow you to, guess what?, yes, **create** and **edit** screen objects, like trim, boxes, lines and fields. **Order** lets you change the tabbing order of the form. **Formattr** and **Location** are mostly concerned with Popup windows so you can research these in your own way.

Save is an important menu option. Well, I never knew that! **Save** is where you make your changes permanent. It is possible to choose the exit option without saving your form; however INGRES is quite well mannered, as you will find in section 6.4.

```
┌─────────────────────────────────────────────────────────────┐
│                       CUSTOMER Table                        │
│                                                             │
│                                                             │
│      Custno: f_____        Custcont: c_____    │
│                                                             │
│    Custname: c_____   Custaddr1: c_____     │
│                                                             │
│   Custaddr2: c_____   Custaddr3: c_____     │
│                                                             │
│     Billing: c_                                             │
│                                                             │
│                                                             │
│                                                             │
│                                                             │
│                                                             │
│                                                             │
│ Create Delete  Edit  Move  Undo  Order  Save  FormAttr  Location  Help  End > │
└─────────────────────────────────────────────────────────────┘
```

Figure 6.2 Default customer form with simple fields

6.3.5 Moving around

Moving around is nice and easy; just use the **tab** key and this will take you from field to field. The arrow keys will take you to parts of the form without an object. You will need this facility to place the cursor for extra lines, boxes and those informative bits of trim, like "Greatest debts of all time" or "Who owes me most money".

6.3.6 Editing trim

To discover the pleasure of screens try Exercise 6.4. If you don't want to "suck it and see" read this section first and then try the exercise.

When you have moved the cursor to a trim object, selecting **Edit** will bring a prompt "Edit trim" on the menu line and the cursor is placed at the first character of the trim. From here you can insert, change or delete characters singly or complete words. A note from our sponsors, to finish editing use the menu key or the return key. You can also move trim, but more of that later. Return may or may not delete the line from the cursor position to the end of the trim. This will depend on how your system has been set up. You can edit trim at any time, returning to change the spelling or punctuation repeatedly.

Exercise 6.4

First, before more dramatic actions, try moving about the cursor around the screen (Tab and Ctrl P usually).

*Now use the cursor movement keys to place the cursor on the heading for the screen. This should read CUSTOMER Table. Select **Edit** to change the heading. To make this form the data entry form for adding new customers, change the heading to "New Customer Entry Form". Don't forget the possible effect of **Return**, blanking the field from the cursor position to the end, and ending the edit. The conventional method of ending editing would be to use the **Menu** key. Try out the effects of both **Return** and **Menu** keys. Do not worry about making mistakes. Selecting **End** without subsequently saving the form will solve that.*

6.3.7 Moving display objects

This is where art takes over! Moving an object is simple. First you move the cursor to the object you want to move, then select the **Move** menu option. The submenu you see contains simple options, like **centre**, **left** and **right**, which move the object to those relative positions on the form.

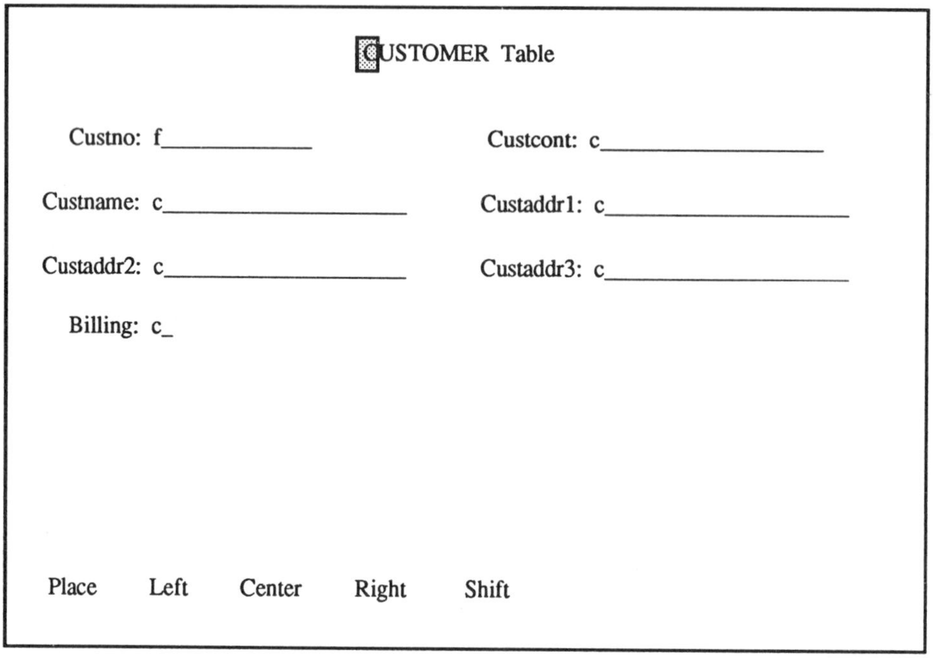

```
CUSTOMER Table


    Custno: f_____        Custcont: c_____


   Custname: c_____    Custaddr1: c_____


  Custaddr2: c_____    Custaddr3: c_____

    Billing: c_






  Place     Left     Center     Right     Shift
```

Figure 6.3 Default form with the Move submenu

If you select **move** and then use the cursor keys to move about the form, selecting **place** or **shift** will move the object to the cursor's position. Fields can be moved as a whole or title and data windows can be moved separately. Each of the parts of fields can be moved using **place**, **centre**, etc. Hours of fun for all the family can be had just with the **Vifred move** option.

Exercise 6.5

Make sure the cursor is still on the heading, because you are going to move the heading to the centre of the screen.

*Select **Move** and look at the submenu now shown, it should look like Figure 6.3. You can choose other options, including **Left** and **Right**, but for the moment take the **Center** option, and watch the result. You can try the other options, but end the editing session with **Center**.*

6.3.8 Deleting trim

An easy option this. After moving the cursor to the object that is not wanted, select the **Delete** option. INGRES is not brain damaged, so it will refuse to let you delete a line on the screen if there are objects on the line. You can't delete a box unless you are exactly on the boxes border. But don't worry or build up stress factors, the **Undo** option will let the previous edit or delete option be rolled back, to before your edit.

Exercise 6.6

Now you are going to create two new lines, and some trim explaining the use of the screen. After all people who are going to use this screen need to know what you want them to do.

*First, **move** the cursor to a blank line immediately below the heading, and then select **Create**. You will be shown a new menu, and you need to choose **NewLine**. As you can see, this command opens up a new line at the cursor position. Repeat this series of commands again, without moving the cursor, and then move the cursor down one line.*

*Now you are going to create a new line of trim. Select **Create**, and then **Trim**. Now the cursor is at the start of your new trim. Make this line of trim read "Enter a new customer's details and select Append". If you want to change the message, carry on, but try to keep instructions simple. Try the **Move** command to move this trim **right** and **left**. You could also try an alternative method of moving trim by putting the cursor where you want the trim to start and press **Place** or **Shift**. Experimentation will help you become more familiar with the action of these commands.*

6.3.9 Editing a field

Editing a field is only more complex than editing trim because there is more to do, title, and fields and things. To edit, gosh this is familiar, move the cursor on to the object and select edit. The submenu gives you a number of options, but for the moment we will look at the field components we have already mentioned earlier in the chapter. Remember that far back? Take a look at Figure 6.4, showing the field edit submenu if you can't remember.

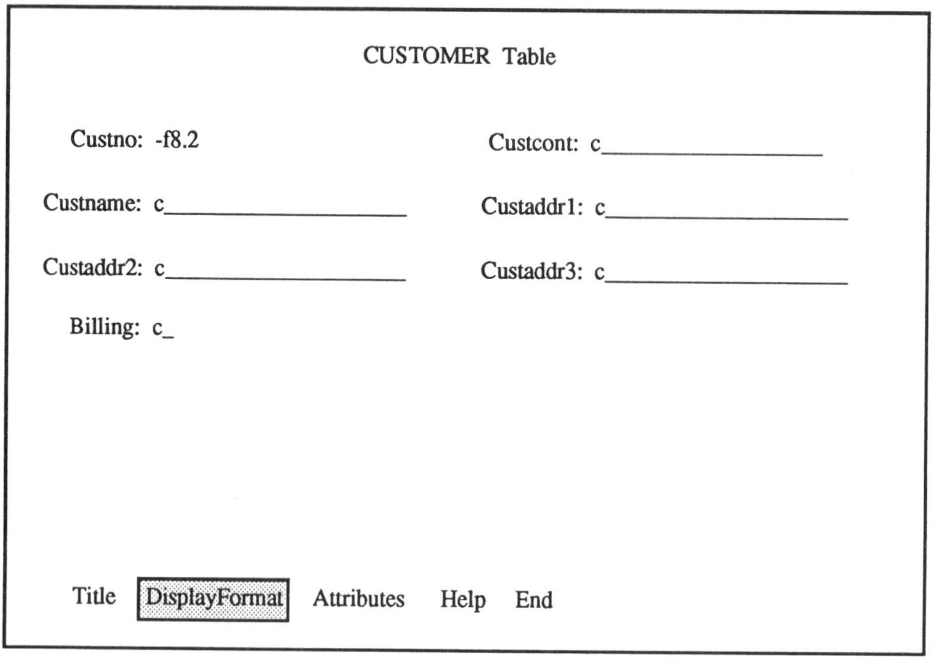

```
┌──────────────────────────────────────────────────────────────┐
│                        CUSTOMER Table                          │
│                                                                │
│                                                                │
│      Custno:  -f8.2              Custcont:  c_____    │
│                                                                │
│    Custname:  c_____    Custaddr1:  c_____   │
│                                                                │
│    Custaddr2:  c_____   Custaddr3:  c_____   │
│                                                                │
│      Billing:  c_                                              │
│                                                                │
│                                                                │
│                                                                │
│                                                                │
│                                                                │
│                                                                │
│       Title  │DisplayFormat│  Attributes    Help    End        │
│                                                                │
└──────────────────────────────────────────────────────────────┘
```

Figure 6.4 Edit data windows

Title
Selecting **Title** from the submenu moves the cursor onto the first character of the title and lets you edit it in the same way as you edit trim.

A little tip: many novice users put trim in front of fields, but each field can have a title. You still need a title, even if you don't want any words; use the delete key to remove title from fields that don't need one. This would typically apply to multiple fields of a similar type. If address is displayed in three fields, then you can delete the title from two fields and move them closer together.

Exercise 6.7

*After changing a field's title the next thing to edit is the data display format. If you have had to stop editing, return to the state that the last exercise left you in. The menu on the bottom of the screen will show you the **Edit** options for data field, select **DisplayFormat**, and change the length of the field from c20 to c30. After doing this end the editing session; remember to use return or the menu key, and select **End** to return to the **Vifred** main menu. Chapter 7 will tell you how to edit the attributes.*

Display Format

Before editing the display format, look at Figure 6.5 you can see c_____ and f____.__ in the data windows of fields. The underscores show show the maximum possible number of display characters. The "c" or "f" tells you if the data window holds character or numeric data. The "f" means that if the corresponding data type is money or a decimal number, to display a decimal point where the dot is. Other letters are: c, character format; d, date format; i, integer; e, scientific notation, and f,g,n are for different types of floating point. A number of examples are shown below in Figure 6.6.

When the **Edit** submenu is chosen and the **DisplayFormat** is selected you are allowed to edit or enter the display format. After your edit you press the menu key to stop. But what do you put in the display format. First, remember that the display format of a field must correspond to the data type of a column in a database table. This is important to remember when you change the data type of a column, or the display format of a field. For example, having a display data format of c10, for ten characters would display 1234, etc. as characters, but this would cause problems in calculation if you tried to treat those characters as digits.

-c6	This would display six or less characters, justified to the left. This is the default alignment.
-f8.2	This would display up to eight digits, six before the decimal point and two after. NOT eight characters before and two after the decimal point. CAUTION! This catches a number of people out.
+i10	This format would display up to ten integer characters, but right aligned.
-d25	The date would be displayed as 25 characters, left aligned.
-d"Feb 3rd 01"	Wow, what a mouthful. This would display the date according to a specific format so that you can specify how different dates are displayed on your form. This would display 29.06.51 as "Jun 29th 51". Date formats are the same in Vifred and RBF (Report by forms). The characters in the format are special characters which are replaced by the data in the column. What the characters are and their effect is explained in the chapter on reports.

Figure 6.5 Examples of editable display formats

When you are editing a form it may not be wise to change the display format except in length until you have gained a little more experience. If you are looking for more detail on this topic, the INGRES Forms and Menus and Report Writer manual has whole chapters on **Vifred**. One final word about the "+" and "-" signs in front of the display format. These are to do with justification. The plus sign will tell INGRES to display data in that window aligned to the right.

Check the examples in Figure 6.5 if you are not sure of the editing effects.

Attributes
Attribute editing is such a big topic that it has a whole chapter to itself, the

next chapter "Improving the functionality". For the moment all you need to do is remember how you get the attribute editing option. Now is the time to attempt Exercise 6.8.

Exercise 6.8

*After changing a field's title the next thing to edit is the data display format. If you have had to stop editing, return to the state that the last exercise left you in. The menu on the bottom of the screen will show you the **Edit** options for data field, select **DisplayFormat**, and change the length of the field from c20 to c30. After doing this end the editing session, and select **End** to return to the **Vifred** main menu. Attributes will be edited in the next chapter.*

6.3.10 Moving fields

Moving fields is easy (tell that to the farmers!). Again the selection of **move** highlights the field and brings a submenu. Don't forget to put the cursor on the field you want to move or **Vifred** may beep at you. The submenu contains the normal quota of options plus **Title** and **Format**. To move the whole field just treat it like trim, and use centre, right, etc. to place the field. The main difference between the way that fields and trim are handled is in the submenu choices, which let you move the title and data window independently. Selecting **title** from the submenu will highlight the title and you can use all the normal options to move the title about the form. This is normally used to place the title above the data window. Likewise selecting **Format** will highlight just the format and let you move this about the screen. Don't be tempted to move field elements too far appart, remember the title is intended to tell you about the data in the field.

6.3.11 Creating boxes and lines

Default forms do not normally have boxes and lines on them, except when a master detail **JoinDef** is used with the tablefield option. This is a special case and those boxes and lines are not for editing, but are under the control of **Vifred**. The boxes and lines that you can create and edit using

Create Box/Line option, when the cursor is on the object, are trim and can be treated as such. Moving boxes and lines and changing their attributes are achieved from the Form layout frame menu. Those of you with a spirit of adventure may have selected the **Attribute** option when editing a field and seen the Box attribute. This is also different from boxes created with **Create Box/Line**.

Placing the cursor where you feel that it is right for a box to start from select **Create** and then **Box/Line**. Remember that boxes and lines are normally used to separate data on a form or group data together, so again use with care and due artistic taste. The cursor has a cross placed on it and you are told to move the cursor to position the opposite corner, using arrow keys, and press the **menu** key when you are done. Creating a line means moving the cursor vertically up or down or horizontally left or right. This in effect creates a box with either no height or no width. Editing boxes follows the same sequence as the other edit options, **place cursor, select edit**, and follow the submenu instructions, however you will see that this edit screen has a different set of submenus. The **Resize** option highlights the upper left-hand corner of the box and places the cursor on the diagonally oposite corner, letting you shrink or expand the box as you wish. The other options are self explanatory. Try Exercise 9, to become more familiar with boxes.

Exercise 6.9

Now is the time to create a box around the address fields on your customer form. Find a sensible place for the address fields to go in a block and move them, one at a time, so that address line 1 comes directly above address line 2, and so on. You can get rid of the titles of the fields or move the title of address line one above the address block. Now, after all that place the cursor above and to one side of the block of address lines and select **Create***. Follow this with* **Box/line** *and move the cursor to the opposite corner of the address block. Press the* **menu** *key to finish creating you box. Now you have a box, how about creating a new line on the form. Don't forget that* **Create Newline** *is different from* **Create Box/Line** *as* **Create NewLine** *produces a blank line and* **Create Box/Line** *puts a new line with a line object on it. Have a try with the* **Edit** *option on the box that you have just created. Make the box flashing, and see if you can stand it for more than a few minutes!*

```
┌─────────────────────────────────────────────────────────────────┐
│                        CUSTOMER Table                             │
│                                                                   │
│      Custno: f_____        Custcont: c_____   │
│                                                                   │
│    Custname: c_____  Custaddr1: c_____  │
│                                                                   │
│    Custaddr2: c_____  Custaddr3: c_____   │
│                                                                   │
│      Billing: c_                                                  │
│                                                                   │
│                                                                   │
│                                                                   │
│                                                                   │
│                                                                   │
│    Trim   Field   TableField   NewLine  │Box/Line│  Help  End     │
│                                                                   │
└─────────────────────────────────────────────────────────────────┘
```

Figure 6.6 Creating boxes

6.4 Saving Forms for Later

After all the time and effort spent on creating an aesthetically pleasing and ergonomically well designed form, it would be a pity if it were lost. So SAVE IT! This involves the **Save** option. If you can't see one on your menu line, try the menu key, and see what is on the line "off the screen". If you still can't see the save option you may need glasses, or you may be in the **Edit** option. Keep using the menu key until you see the **Save** option, but don't be tempted to try and **Quit**. I know that INGRES is another of those irritating pieces of software that asks you "Do you really want to quit? Do you really really really want to quit?" ad infinitum. In this case INGRES is justified in its questions. If you select **Quit**, and say that you don't want to save your form, INGRES will assume that you know what you are doing (foolish assumption eh?) and your edit session will be lost.

Selecting **Save** will give you the **Save** frame, see Figure 6.7. You can put in a name to save the form under, a short remark to be displayed with the name in the catalog frame, and a more explanatory long remark which will give information to those who come after you, or to yourself if you are forgetful. After completing the save frame to your satisfaction, select **Save** again and you will be returned to the catalogs frame. This is where your form is saved. When you have saved successfully and returned to the catalog frame you will see your form details displayed in the catalog frame.

Exercise 6.10

*When you are satisfied that your form has broken new ground, artistically, select the **Save** menu choice. If you cannot find it on your current screen, read section 6.4 again. If you have successfully saved your form, take a rest.*

6.4.1 QBFNames

When you save a form that will be used to query the database it is saved by name, and that name is the default QBFname of the form. The QBFname is the identifier that links a Vifred form with a particular database table or **JoinDef**. To use a form that you have edited you should use the QBFnames option in QBF. Vifred will not allow you to access the database itself; don't forget it is an editor. Referring to the QBFname of the form will give you the tailored form, rather than a default. QBFnames can be changed by using the **QBFnames** option from the **Utilities** option of the Vifred catalogs frame.

6.4.2 Long and short remarks

Don't neglect these facilities in saving or editing a form, as they can save, if not your life, perhaps your job. Badly documented software is always expensive and difficult to maintain. If you include details in the short and long remarks about the function and logic behind the use of the form then you have given another user a head start in understanding what the form is about. End of sermon, on with the rest of the book.

```
VIFRED - Saving a Form

   Name : customer                          Created: 12-apr-1990 12:23:00

   Owner : petem                            Modified:  12-apr-1990 13:43:18

Short Remark :  Calls system customer form

Long Remark :
   ┌─────────────────────────────────────────────────────────────────────────┐
   │ Telephone calls monitoring system Basic customer form                     │
   │ Mostly for customer data entry. Validation for Customer name and number mandatory │
   │                                                                           │
   │                                                                           │
   │                                                                           │
   └─────────────────────────────────────────────────────────────────────────┘

Save     Format    Help
```

Figure 6.7 Form **Save** frame

6.5 Style and Usage of Fields

6.5.1 General pomposity

You may remember, a few sentences ago I said "End of sermon"? Well I lied, because here I continue in the same fashion. Although **Vifred** gives you all these facilities, like flashing different colour boxes, etc., don't use them all at once! Remember, it may be fun and look good to you, but some poor sucker may have to spend 8 hours a day looking at it. In general leave the flashing lights to the security services, or the control of the 4GL. Flashing form objects should be used to notify the user of an unusual error or condition, not a regular occurrence. And finally a word from our sponsor: Beware of the joke heading and trim on your form. It wouldn't be the first time that someone has gone on vacation and the form, including the joke header, has been used in a production system. Keep those jobs, folks!

6.5.2 Cursor movement

Default order
Every field has a default order to it, that is the order in which the cursor moves from field to field. This is usually the order in which the columns details are placed on the default form. This may not be the order in which you wish to use the form, so INGRES has given you the option to change the order of the fields.

Changing the order
Selecting **Order** from the Vifred form editing main menu, as shown in Figure 6.2, will give you a display which has the fields, and the current tabbing order, as seen in Figure 6.9. The submenu contains a few options that you may be familiar with. **Forget** is an option that you will find handy, as it will cancel any changes and return you to the layout menu. This is especially useful if you have got yourself into trouble on a complex form and feel that it is best to restart from the beginning. **DefaultOrder** will perform a similar function, in that it will restore the default order of the form, but doesn't take you back to the main menu. **Edit** is the option you take, when your cursor is on a field you wish to change. You simply type in the new number of the field, and press the menu key. You must then go and change another number, as you are not allowed to save the changes by selecting **End** until there are unique field numbers on the form. INGRES will tell you, if you have forgotten, and won't let you end. You may want to try Exercise 6.11 after section 6.6, so that you know how to test your forms first.

```
┌─────────────────────────────────────────────────────────────┐
│                      CUSTOMER  Table                        │
│                                                             │
│                                                             │
│       Custno: 1                    Custcont: 2              │
│                                                             │
│     Custname: 3                   Custaddr1: 4              │
│                                                             │
│    Custaddr2: 5                   Custaddr3: 6              │
│                                                             │
│       Billing: 7                                            │
│                                                             │
│                                                             │
│                                                             │
│                                                             │
│                                                             │
│     Edit   DefaultOrder   Forget   Help   End              │
│                                                             │
└─────────────────────────────────────────────────────────────┘
```

Figure 6.8 Tabbing order

Exercise 6.11

*Now is the time to try out the cursor movement order. Select the **Edit** option from the **Vifred** catalog frame, after moving the cursor onto the form that you saved in Exercise 10. Select **Order** and view the form shown. Change the numbers that you can see on the screen to move the cursor about. Don't forget that a cursor should move from field to field in a logical manner, and not leap from top to bottom of the screen. Save the form under a new name, by putting in a new name after taking the **Save** option. Try the form out with QBF and see the new order of cursor movement. When you have finished return to the **Vifred** catalog.*

6.6 Testing your Forms

Testing your forms, before using them in anger, is sensible, and will give you hours of pleasure and frustration. Vifred does not let you directly test your forms; it is after all an editor, not a database access tool. You must use QBF or 4GL to test your forms. QBF is simpler, and 4GL is not covered in detail in this book, so the choice is easy.

6.6.1 Using QBFnames

We have already mentioned QBFnames and their significance, but you must remember that to test the form you must use QBFnames rather than the table name.

6.6.2 Calling QBF from Vifred

This is one of the really useful improvements in version 6 INGRES, as previously you had to exit from Vifred completely and call QBF fresh. Now all you need to do is save the form that you have been editing and quit the layout frame. This should present you with the Vifred catalog frame. Place the cursor on the name of your form and select **Go**. QBF will check that there is a valid QBFname and starts QBF with that name as the query target. Then all you do is use QBF menu options to see your form in action. After you have finished, exit from QBF and you will be returned to Vifred, ready to edit or exit from the catalog's frame.

6.7 Multiple Tables

6.7.1 JoinDefs

One of the great tricks of Vifred is to create a form using a **JoinDef** as the default form. The underlying functionality of the **JoinDef** remains intact, any joins and rules specified stay the same, but a form saved from a **JoinDef** default has all the additional appearance and functionality that Vifred gives you. If you look at Figure 6.10 you will see a default form for a JoinDef.

Exercise 6.12

*Time for the clever stuff. You are going to get and edit a **JoinDef**. When asked for a **JoinDef** name, enter the name of the **JoinDef** that you created in the exercises of Complex Data Manipulation. First make any changes to trim and simple fields that you would like. Now, without doing any more to the form, read the next section of the chapter.*

6.7.2 Table fields

This section will show you how to specify table fields. Before moving on to look in more details at table fields, can you remember the description used to define table fields? No, shame on you; try reading this book in the morning, then you won't go to sleep. A couple of clues: do the words multiple rows, scrolling, and data set mean anything to you? If you are really baffled, try the previous chapter.

Table fields, although they display many rows at one time on a screen, giving you a window onto a data set, can be treated as a single object for some Vifred actions.

Moving
To move a table field use the tab key to place the cursor on the top corner of the table field. **Move** and **move, centre, right,** etc. are the options, just like moving a simple field.

Exercise 6.13

Place the cursor onto the table field, and select move. Move the table field up a few lines. Centre the table field. Don't leave this form for the moment as you will need it for the next exercise.

Internal Names

The internal name of the table field is always supplied by Vifred, when you use a **JoinDef** default form. To see the internal name of a form, place the cursor anywhere on a table field and select **Edit**. The name of the tablefield is the internal name, by which 4GL code differentiates between columns on a table field and simple fields. Do not change this name, unless you want to make it more meaningful. If you make a mistake, there is always the opportunity to **Forget** the editing, and return to the default.

No. of rows to display

The number of rows displayed is specified in this field; the default is four. You can change this to 99, but usually it is best only to display a number that can be held on one screen. There is also a **Display Lines(y/n)** field. This will display lines between rows, but as each line takes up the same space as a row, you will halve the number of rows you can display. However it is useful for separating rows of important information.

Highlight current row

This is a useful option, letting you select the highlighting of a row when the cursor is placed on a table field. When you are using the form, via QBF, placing the cursor on the table field, and using the cursor keys to move up and down will cause each row the cursor moves to be displayed in inverse video. This function is only available through Vifred. Replace the "y" in the field with an "n" and you switch this function off.

Column titles

Use of "n" in the Display Column Titles?(y/n) field will stop the titles of the columns being displayed. This is handy for using some of the special effects of trim, and **Box/Line**. Normally you will leave this field at the default, "y", as the QBF opportunities are limited, but there are some interesting effects in 4GL, especially with pop-up frames, that can make your forms really glitzy!

To change the column title move the cursor to that title and make your changes. One thing to remember though: INGRES will shorten your title if you make it too long. For example a title of "Repayments Charge Indicator" for a field that is only 4 characters long will come out at

"Repay", or near enough. You will get your chance to see all this in Exercise 6.13.

```
┌─────────────────────────────────────────────────────────────────────┐
│                        CALL  Table                                    │
│                                                                       │
│                                                                       │
│       Call Id : f_____              Custno:  f_____            │
│                                                                       │
│       Operat Id : c _____         Start Tm : d_____       │
│                                                                       │
│       End Tm : d_____                                           │
│                                                                       │
│                                                                       │
│    CALL_DETAILS TABLE(S):                                             │
│   ┌──────────────┬──────────────┬─────────────────────────────────┐  │
│   │ Equip Id     │  Action Id   │           Description            │  │
│   │ c_____     │ c_____  │ c_____│ │
│   │              │              │                                  │  │
│   │              │              │                                  │  │
│   └──────────────┴──────────────┴─────────────────────────────────┘  │
│ Create  Delete  Edit  Move  Undo  Order  Save  FormAttr  Location  Help  End > │
└─────────────────────────────────────────────────────────────────────┘
```

Figure 6.9 Edit JoinDefs

Column Internal Name
The column internal name is the name by which INGRES links the data in a table to the field on a form. Do not edit this name, unless you want to get an entirely different result from the one you expected. The prize of a restful night's sleep is yours if you can guess when you may want to use this facility to edit a name, before reading the next sentence. Too late, it is used when you change the column name in a table and want to use the form without going through all that editing again.

Display format
The display format of a field is the same here as it is for a simple field. A

description of how the data in a column is going to be displayed. It follows the same rules about editing., etc, as simple fields display formats.

GetTableDef
This is an important menu option; all the others displayed are self explanatory by now, I hope. Rather than individually entering column titles, display formats, etc. when you are creating a table field, you can use the existing tables in the database to provide default entries by selecting **GetTabledef** and letting INGRES do the work for you. I won't go into detail here, as we are talking about editing default forms, but you will find this function useful when you create from a blank form.

Exercise 6.13

*Unless you tried anything else after the previous exercise, you should be looking at a form created from a **JoinDef**. Move the cursor to the table field and select **Edit**. From here change the number of rows displayed and edit the column headings to look more presentable. What happens when you put a column heading larger than the display field? Edit some of the display fields, if you wish, and edit the order in which they are displayed. Use **End** to exit the table field editing form. Try out your form and **Exit** from **Vifred** when you have finished.*

6.8 Pop-up forms

A pop-up form is very similar to a normal **Vifred** form in that it is created in the same way, and all the commands associated with it are identical, but it differs mostly in use. I am including it here for information's sake, because no matter how hard you try, you can't use pop-up forms, except in 4GL or an embedded language. Their action can only be controlled in that way; there is no facility to use them in QBF. They are primarily used to provide a "window" function, leaving the existing form on the screen and being overlaid on top of it. All the normal actions from menus can be used and processing of the underlying frame is suspended for the duration of the use of the pop-up. Further information on the use of pop-ups and the code to control them can be gleaned from INGRES manuals.

6.9 Using the Create Option on Blank Forms

This option will allow you to create an entire form from a blank. All you have to remember is to use the create, rather than the edit option. After sufficient practice with editing default forms, so you are familiar with all the object types, and the menu functions, you should be able to create a form easily enough. However, most forms can be created from table and **JoinDef** defaults in the simple systems.

6.10 Chapter Review

In this chapter you have covered the following topics:

o   Editing default forms

o   Creating, editing and moving trim

o   Creating, editing and moving simple fields

o   Creating, editing and moving tablefields

o   Field formats

o   Deleting form objects

o   Saving forms

o   Creating and editing blank forms

6.11 Quick Reference

Create Table Default

- Start **Vifred** on your database

- Select **Create**

- Select **Table**default

- Decide on Simple fields or table fields and select the appropriate option

Create a Join Default

- Start **Vifred** on your database

- Select **Create**

- Select **Join**default

- Decide on simple fields or table fields and select the appropriate option

Edit Trim

- Move the cursor to the trim to be edited

- Select **Edit**

- Make the changes to the trim

- End the edit using **Menu** or **Return** keys

Edit Field

- Move cursor to field

- Select **Edit**

- Select **Title**, make changes and end edit with **Menu** or **Return** key

- Select **DisplayFormat**, make changes and end edit with **Menu** or Return key

Chapter 7

Improving the Functionality

7.1 What You Can and Can't Do with Vifred

This chapter follows on from the last, this chapter completes the work on **Vifred** and gives you the ability to create some truly wonderful and useful customized screens. Remember the sermon from the last chapter? It still applies. Every object and attribute that you create will be on your screen, so no derogatory trim about the chairman, eh?

    Vifred, like all the tools that are included in this book is one of the "quick and dirty" ways of producing an application. Quick and dirty is a familiar term for tools that give high productivity with some lack of flexibility. I would hope that you will agree that you can do a great deal with these tools. However there are some sophistications that you can get with a fully programmed application that you can't get with **Vifred**. For example, in **Vifred** you can specify a field as blinking, but it will blink for as long as the screen in displayed. In most applications you would switch the blinking on and off to signify the arrival or absence of important data. If the sales have fallen below your target, you may want the figure highlighted, for instance. This switching on and off of display attributes cannot be accomplished by **Vifred**. Still, don't be discouraged, there are a lot of things that you can do, including some pretty clever validation and data entry handling.

7.2 How to Change Attributes

Attributes are changed by using the **edit attributes** option, and making some changes on a menu screen displayed. These changes which range from making a selection of attributes to keying in validation error messages are going to be examined in more detail throughout this chapter. We will not discuss all the attributes, as that would make this a list, but in this chapter I will highlight the important functions that these attributes can be used for.

```
┌──────────────────────────────────────────────────────────────────────┐
│  VIFRED - Attributes for Field                                         │
│                              Data Type : varchar        Nullable : y   │
│  ┌──────────────────────┬──────┐                                       │
│  │ Attribute            │ Set  │   Default Value for Field :           │
│  ├──────────────────────┼──────┤                                       │
│  │ Box Field            │  n   │                                       │
│  │ Keep Previous Value  │  n   │   Internal Name for Field             │
│  │ Mandatory Field      │  n   │        Custaddr1                      │
│  │ Reverse Video        │  n   │                                       │
│  │ Blinking             │  n   │   Validation Check to Perform on Field :│
│  │ Underline            │  n   │                                       │
│  │ Brightness Change    │  n   │                                       │
│  │ Query Only           │  n   │                                       │
│  │ Force Lower Case     │  n   │                                       │
│  │ Force Upper Case     │  n   │                                       │
│  │ No Auto Tab          │  n   │   Validation Error Message:           │
│  │ No Echo              │  n   │                                       │
│  │ Display Only         │  n   │   Color :  0                          │
│  │ END OF ATTRIBUTES    │      │                                       │
│  └──────────────────────┴──────┘   Scrollable?(y/n): n                │
│                                                                        │
│  Next    Previous    Help    End                                       │
└──────────────────────────────────────────────────────────────────────┘
```

Figure 7.1 Edit attributes frame

7.2.1 How to get there

During the exercises in the last chapter you will have seen the submenu for editing fields, which allowed you to edit the title and display format, also had an attribute option. You will never guess which option you need to select to make changes to attributes. That's right, the attributes option. Give yourself a prize! Selecting the attributes option from the submenu shows a screen like that displayed in Figure 7.1. Simple changes can be effected by changing 'n' to 'y' and vice versa, in the table of attributes on the left-hand part of the screen. Try Exercise 7.1 for a better understanding of the easy part.

Exercise 7.1

*This exercise takes you to the edit screen for the **Vifred** form that you first created in the previous chapter.*

*Start **Vifred** (if you can't remember how, look in the quick reference at the end of the previous chapter). Move the cursor onto the name of the form created for use with the customer table and select **Edit**.*

*Once you have the form for the customer table on the screen move the cursor to the customer_id field and select **Edit**. The submenu will give you the by now familiar options. Select **attributes** and examine the screen. Make the Customer_id field show in **reverse** video, by moving the cursor to the appropriate position on the attribute box and entering 'y'. Test this out by ending the edit and see what effect it has on the field on the form. Select **edit attributes** again, and carry on with the chapter until the next exercise.*

7.2.2 Next and previous

If you look at the submenu in Figure 7.1 you will see two options **Next** and **Previous**. These options are used to allow you to edit all of the simple fields on the form, without all this end edit, tab to next field, start new edit, end edit, etc. Pressing the key associated with **Next** will display the "Attributes for Field" screen for the next field in the tabbing order. The tabbing order has been set by default, but you can change it. Check the **Order** section in the previous chapter. Selecting **Previous** will have the opposite effect. In this way you can edit a series of fields without having to return to the main **Vifred** editing screen.

7.3 Display Attributes

Most of the attributes that we examine in this section of the chapter are set or unset by putting a 'y' or an 'n' in the set column opposite the corresponding name in the attribute column. Read the name and the set value carefully, as there are a couple of double negatives in there. The default value for attribute settings is 'n'.

7.3.1 Changing the colour of a field

If you are one of the chosen, using a colour terminal, it is possible to change the colour of a field, for more emphasis, by tabbing the cursor to the **colour** area on the attributes form and type in a new colour number. If you don't know what colours are represented by the normal numbers 0 to 7 then some experimentation will help. There is a set of sample equivalents in the manual.

7.3.2 Previous values

The **Keep Previous Value** attribute will display the previously entered value in the field with this attribute set to 'y'. This is especially good if you are entering a large amount of similar data, like addresses. This attribute in the town or country field will allow you, once you have entered a value, to tab over that entry without changing it, unless you want to. The field then takes the new value which is the value displayed from then on. This is different from a default value, which will be discussed later in the chapter.

7.3.3 Mandatory field

Making the field **mandatory** means that you cannot exit from an append or update operation without a value in this field. INGRES will not let you move from this field without entering some data, when you are using it from **QBF**, for example. The only exception to this is in retrievals, as you are not sending data to the table. This function is particularly good for making sure that people enter vital data, like customer account numbers.

Exercise 7.2

*You should be looking at an Attributes for Field frame. Select **Next** until the internal name for the field tells you that you are editing the **Name** field of the customer form. Don't worry if you go past it. Press **Previous** and you will soon return to the right form.*

    Make name mandatory, and blinking. End your edit of the attributes and examine the screen you are then presented with. It should show the data window for the name field winking at you. This can get a little wearing, having a constantly flashing screen in front of you, to say nothing of migraine sufferers heading for the pill cabinet. Re-edit the attributes for customer name, and stop that #$@@!?! blinking. Leave your terminal for the moment and carry on with the next part of the chapter.

7.3.4 Query only

The **query only** attribute sets the form up to allow the person using the form with **QBF** to enter data in the field for retrieval, but no data can be entered in an append mode. You can use this on a copy of a form that is used for data entry to ensure that changes can't be made to this field, but you can still retrieve based on values in the field. Payroll or accounting forms would use this facility, letting a payroll clerk retrieve a range of bonus values, but not alter them.

Exercise 7.3

Use next and previous to make the address lines 1, 2 and 3 query only and then carry on with the rest of the chapter.

7.3.5 Display only

This option is even more restrictive than query only, as it only lets the user see what is in the field; the user can't even tab to the field to put in a query parameter. If you look at the tabbing order of the fields after setting this attribute on a field, you will see that there is no order number for display only fields.

7.3.6 Blinking, underline and brightness changes

Well, these are the tricky ones, aren't they? All this group of attributes do is change the look of the display, but remember the many pompous sermons from the last chapter? Use these functions sparingly, as some poor sucker, it may even be you, will be looking at these screens for hours a day.

7.3.7 Upper and lower cases

If you have a field on the form that must be all upper or lower case, setting this attribute will force the data entered into the corresponding case. I find this particularly useful for enforcing some sort of standard on important keys, like surnames. It makes life easier if you don't have to use complex wildcards to get all of the data from the file.

Exercise 7.4

*Move to **edit** the attributes of the billing code field, and make this field **upper case**. If you want to experiment with any of the other attributes, now is the time. After you are satisfied with the attributes that you have changed and the overall appearance of the form is like mother used to make, **save** the form. Don't forget to use a sensible name and enter any short comments that will help to understand the form's functions.*

Now you have saved the form you should be looking at the form's catalog frame. This is the place to run the form through QBF. When you are looking at the form there are a number of things you can try. You should attempt to enter items or use parts of the form that you have restricted using **Vifred**. *A good example of this is to use the form in* **append** *mode and fill in all the fields except the* **name**. *INGRES should then tell you that you have made a mistake, as the name field is mandatory, or should be if you completed Exercise 7.2 properly. Get the idea? You can try entering lower case billing codes, etc. When you are happy with the work so far return to the* **Vifred** *catalog frame.*

7.3.8 No autotab

If you have not spotted the trick question, have another look at the attribute screen display in Figure 7.1. Just what does 'No Auto Tab', 'n' mean? Well I am sure that you have worked it out as 'Yes, let's auto tab', but what does it mean? An auto tab attribute, set by default will move the cursor from the end of one field onto the next field in the tabbing order, when the field is full. If this is set to 'y' auto tab is set off, and the cursor stays on the field, even if it is full up.

7.3.9 No echo

This is another of the double negatives, as the default setting is 'n', meaning 'yes, echo character'. Changing this attribute is especially handy if you are editing a form that is going to have some measure of security added, like a password. This attribute set to 'y' will not display characters in the field, even as you key them in. A little something for all you cold warriors out there, perhaps?

7.4 Validation Attributes

One of the most important functions of the attributes screen is the ability to enter data validation instructions quickly and easily. This will really make a difference to the impact of your forms.

Operator	Description
=	Equal to
!=	Not equal to
<>	Not equal to
<	Less than
<=	Less than or equal to
>	Greater than
>=	Greater than or equal to
LIKE	SQL string equal to

Figure 7.2 Table of comparison operators

Validation checks are defined by the designer of the form and consist of either a comparison with a set of details or a comparison using operators. An operator is an symbol that specifies what sort of check to make, for example the right arrow '>' means greater than in the context A>B, A is greater than B. If you are unsure about operators, especially the Boolean operators, check the INGRES through Forms and Menus and Report Writer manual. In this section we will look at comparisons made using operators

7.4.1 Comparisons

This is where you would specify the value that has been typed in the field whose attributes you are editing. For example, you can use the statement 'customer_ref > 2000' to make sure that no value less than or equal to 2000 can be entered in this field. In the event that a person enters 1999 in the customer_ref field **Vifred** will detect it and give an error message. You can type in your own error message, up to 50 characters in the Validation Error Message field. This will be displayed on encountering the validation error and should be informative. In the case of a customer_ref less than or equal to 2000 the message could read 'Customer reference must be greater than 2000. Try again'. Comparisons should be in the format below.

```
fieldname compop constant
```

no_in_stock > 0	If a value is entered in the no_in_stock column it must be greater than zero, any other value will give an error
reorder_level >= 0	If a value is entered in the re-order column it must be greater than or equal to zero
price < 1000	Any value entered in the price column must be less than 1000 units.
no_in_stock <= 50	The no_in_stock entry should be less than or equal to 50

Figure 7.3 Examples of comparison formats

There are other formats but they will be looked at in the section on Nulls. Fieldname in this case is the name of the field whose attributes you are editing. The term *compop* is used for comparison operator, as in Figure 7.2. Finally a constant is a constant value that is put into the form definition and can only be changed by re-editing the form's attributes. A few examples of these formats and their effects are shown in Figure 7.3.

Exercise 7.5

*Start **Vifred** on a simple field table default of the Equipment table. Edit the attributes of the **unit_cost** field to ensure that it will not allow entry of zero or less.*

7.4.2 Character strings

Character strings can be used as constants in a comparison, but there are a few rules. If you can think of anywhere there aren't rules, answers on a postcard please. The character string for comparison must be enclosed in double quotes, except when you are using the LIKE operator. For example, in the equipment table is a column called location, so if location always had to have a "W" as the first character this could be ensured with the following statement typed into the validation statement field.

        location = "W*"

This not only uses a string, but introduced a wildcard. Do you remember those little beasties from the QBF sections? You can use wildcards for a number of characters, one character or a range of characters, in the same way that QBF wildcards are used. A few examples of the use of character strings and wildcards are shown in Figure 7.4.

Exercise 7.6

*Move to the **location** field and since all the stock has to be kept in a warehouse, make sure that the location always starts with upper case W. While you are there make the location field force upper case with a default of **W1**, but keep the previous value.*

7.4.3 Date and money validation

Date and money abstract data types are validated in the same way as character comparisons, by being enclosed in double quotes. For example, to check if the date is later than 1st October 1989 you would use date > "1-Oct-1989".

location = "W*"	Here any location that is entered must have an upper case W to start
address = "B*s"	In this case the address must start with an upper case B and end with a lower case s.
name like 'C*' name like '*s'	Notice the single quotes here, this means that you are making an SQL comparison using the like operator. Using like is the same as using an equals sign, but you must use a single quote.

Figure 7.4 Character string comparisons

7.4.4 Oh no! Nulls again

Yes, here they are again, but in validations. To compare for the null value use IS NULL, as in price IS NULL. Conversely to compare for any value but not the null value, yes you've guessed, IS NOT NULL is used. There are some rules that govern their usage, but at the moment I would suggest that you leave them until you are ready to use nulls in anger. You can find the rules in the INGRES Forms and Menus and Report Writer manual, in the **Vifred** section.

7.4.5 Boolean operators

During this section so far we have looked at simple comparisons, a = 12, date >"1-Feb-1990", and so on. Occasionally there is a need to use more complex validation, by giving alternative validations, for example

price > 20000 and price < 40000

This would give a valid answer if the price input was in the range of less than 20000 and greater than 40000. The monetary units, are of course set by the INGRES name II_MONEY_FORMAT. This would be an environment variable or logical depending on your system. Depending how your system has been set the figures could be in pounds sterling, dollars or escudos.

And, or, not are boolean operators, as you may remember from the QBF chapters, and allow flexibility in validation. The use of parentheses gives even greater flexibility. Parentheses also make comparisons more readable, as all the comparisons inside must be evaluated before other comparisons are evaluated.

In our exercise database the equipment table has a number of dependencies. To give a good example of the use of boolean operators and parentheses, we will suppose that we are designing a screen that will allow us to enter a number of items to be withdrawn from stock, as an order. The number that can be withdrawn depends on the number of stock items left after withdrawal being equal or greater than the re-order level. This condition can be overridden by the user first entering "PRIORITY" into the order_class field. (How would you force the word PRIORITY to be entered as upper case?) As long as this is a priority class order and there are enough stock items held, then the number for withdrawal against the order is allowed. The statement to permit the order number field to be validated against these conditions would look like this:

```
(no_order_items < no_in_stock - reorder_level) or
     (no_order_items => no_in_stock and order_class
     LIKE "PRIORITY")
```

In this example as long as one of the parenthesized conditions is true then the validation is passed. This example also includes some other concepts, such as comparing values in one field on the form with the values in other form fields. We will look at this in the next section. The example shows that you can also subtract values from field values and use the result in a validation. Whilst this is an artificial example, it can be seen here that either one or the other set of validation conditions in the parentheses must be fulfilled, and the use of parentheses makes this more easily readable and understandable.

7.5 Comparisons with Other Objects

Until now we have been concentrating mostly on validation comparisons between a field contents and a value, like a constant or a constant with some wildcards. As the last example has shown there is more to this validation game than we have shown so far. You can compare field contents with the contents of another field, to a list of values, or the contents of a table. Maths is allowed, so it is possible to check a field's value against the contents of another field, minus a constant number or even the number held in yet another field. Confused? You won't be if you watch the next instalment of "Comparisons II - The Movie".

7.5.1 Comparing with other fields

To compare one field with another simply key the field for validation and an operator, followed by the field whose contents are to be used in the validation, as in the example below.

```
fieldname compop otherfieldname
```

Otherfieldname is a field on the form against which you can make comparisons using the operator that replaces *compop*. This is useful if you need to establish some dependency in your form. As an example consider the situation of the no_order_items field in section 7.4.5.

Exercise 7.7

Move to the price field and edit the attributes so that price entered must be greater than or equal to unit cost. If you really wanted to turn a healthy profit you could force the price entered to be greater than ten times the unit cost.

7.5.2 Comparing with a list of values

In Figure 7.5 the field order_class contains the word PRIORITY. It is often useful to make sure that data conforms to an infrequently changing list of values. It may be that order class has only three classes, PRIORITY, NORMAL, OTHER. To make sure that order_class has one of those values we can use the validation statement shown in Figure 7.5:

```
order_class in ["PRIORITY", "NORMAL", "OTHER"]
```

The elements of the list must be separated by commas, and the list should be enclosed in square brackets if they are character constants. The values in the list should be the same data type as the field that you are checking, for example the order_class field should be a character or varchar data type. Numeric constants can be used, and of course would not need the double quotes around them. The keyword **in** tells INGRES that the values following are a list.

A logical extension from this is the idea that a list can be contained in a table. This is a relational database system, you know. The use of lookup tables is described in the next section.

Exercise 7.8

Move to the stock bin field, the only valid entries here are 9, 10, 11 and 12 as the bin numbers in each location. Make that the basis of your validation. Try out your validations by entering incorrect values, after you have saved the form and started it under QBF.

```
┌──────────────────────────────────────────────────────────────────────┐
│  VIFRED - Attributes for Field                                         │
│                              Data Type : varchar        Nullable : y   │
│  ┌─────────────────────┬──────┐                                       │
│  │ Attribute           │ Set  │   Default Value for Field :            │
│  ├─────────────────────┼──────┤                                       │
│  │ Box Field           │ n    │                                       │
│  │ Keep Previous Value │ n    │   Internal Name for Field             │
│  │ Mandatory Field     │ n    │       order_class                     │
│  │ Reverse Video       │ n    │                                       │
│  │ Blinking            │ n    │   Validation Check to Perform on Field : │
│  │ Underline           │ n    │                                       │
│  │ Brightness Change   │ n    │   order_class in ["PRIORITY","NORMAL", │
│  │ Query Only          │ n    │   "OTHER"]                            │
│  │ Force Lower Case    │ n    │                                       │
│  │ Force Upper Case    │ y    │   Validation Error Message:           │
│  │ No Auto Tab         │ n    │   Valid order classes are PRIORITY,NORMAL,OTHER │
│  │ No Echo             │ n    │                                       │
│  │ Display Only        │ n    │   Color :  0                          │
│  │ END OF ATTRIBUTES   │      │                                       │
│  └─────────────────────┴──────┘   Scrollable?(y/n): n                 │
│                                                                        │
│  Next    Previous    Help    End                                       │
└──────────────────────────────────────────────────────────────────────┘
```

Figure 7.5 List of values and attributes

7.5.3 Using lookup tables

Taking the example of order_class in the preceding system having three values in a list, what would happen if the three values changed frequently or there were 200 values? Remember that you are only allowed 200 characters in the validation statement and to change a constant you have to edit the attributes of the form again. If you have a good memory, now is where you scream "You told us in the last section, Bozo!", because I did tell you.

A lookup table is an ordinary database table which contains a list of values that can be referred to in the validation statement by using this expression:

```
fieldname in tablename.columnname
```

This causes the forms runtime system to read the database table named in tablename, and make a list of the data in columnname. This list is held in the computer's memory, and is not changed until the form has been quit and re-started. Any changes to the database table do not appear in the list until it has been read again, by starting QBF on that form.

This is very useful for lists of values that change frequently. All you need to do is change the table contents and the list is updated next time QBF is started. Large lists can also be accommodated by this method, but beware, the larger the list the longer it takes for INGRES to start QBF as it has a big table to read first. If you placed the order_class values in a database table called classifications you could do a table lookup validation using the following statement.

```
order_class in classifications.order_class
```

It is important that you separate the tablename and columnname by a dot, and you must always put both of them in. **Vifred** won't tell you that you have it wrong until you save the form, and then it will give you a chance to make the change interactively.

Exercise 7.9

You are going to create a different **Vifred** *form, on the joindef you produced in Exercises 5.4 onwards. It will be used for logging calls. If you followed my advice in the text you called the JoinDef* **call_in_j**. *Once you are comfortably looking at your form edit the attributes of the* **operator_id** *to display the previous value.*

Edit the attributes of **start_time** *to be a default of "now". Edit the attributes of the* **operator_id** *to make sure that you can only enter operators that are in the operator_id field of the operator's table. Remember to use the "dot" to separate tables and columns.*

7.6 Display Formats

The option to change display formats is in this chapter, rather than the edit display formats section of the previous chapter, as this is definitely an improvement in the functionality, as a date displayed as 14th June 1990 would possibly be easier to read than 06.14.1990. When we are discussing display formats, remember you should not be looking at the Field attributes screen, but the **Vifred** editing form, on which all the fields and their positions are displayed.

Display Format	Effect
+c5	Will display, left justified five character maximum. If the data to be displayed is longer than the number of characters then the extra character won't be displayed, although they are still there. For example Williams displayed in this format would be Willi.
-i3	Will display integer, float or money as a field of three digits. If you try and display an integer larger than three digits Ingres will fill the field with asterisks. The data is not lost, but can't be seen, so the field will need to be increased in size.
-f6.2	This will force a number to be displayed in a field that is six characters long, including the decimal point. So a maximum of five digits will be displayed. The number 2 at the end signifies the number of digits to be displayed after the decimal point. The minus sign forces data to be right justified.

Figure 7.6 Examples of display formats and their effects

One important point about changing the default display formats. You must make sure that the new format is compatible with the data type of the field. If you change the data format to an incompatible data type **Vifred** thinks you know what you are doing, and changes the field's data type to match. This could cause you problems if you retrieve a data item

"The Old House" from the customer table into a field expecting 23.44.

To save this section being merely a reprint of the manual we will only look at the more common data formats. One point all the data formats have in common is the use of plus(+) and minus(-) signs for justification. If a plus sign precedes a data format it causes the data to be displayed, aligned to the left. A tricky question that you will never answer: Where is data aligned if the first character in a data format is a minus sign? If you really can't work this one out, shame on you, but look at the examples in Figure 7.6. There are some neat tricks that you can do with long lines and multiple lines, but they are better looked at in the manual, after you have mastered the basics.

7.6.1 Character data

Character data includes any of the character data types (varchar, char, c, text). As you may remember from the previous chapter the default format for character data display is -cN. The minus sign we have already covered. The **c** stands for character, and the N in this case represents the number of characters to be displayed. This would default to the size of the character column if you created the form from a table or JoinDef default. There are many things you can do, for example -c80.20 would display a maximum of 80 characters on four lines of 20 characters each, great for long addresses. Check out the use of the f and j parameters in the manual, if you are likely to do a lot of this sort of formatting.

If you set a field's format to be c10 and the related column width is 40 characters, don't despair, as you can make the field **scrollable** by tabbing down to the bottom of the attributes for field form, where you find the field labelled "Scrollable(y/n)?". Entering a "y" here will allow you to set the field scroll size. The scroll size is the underlying width of the field, so you can make the size 40 characters, although only ten characters appear on the screen at any one time. To see other characters in a scrollable field use the left and right arrow keys. Entering data is easy, you just keep typing. Only one word of caution. This facility is restricted to **unjustified** character display formats, which is why I had not put the justification sign in front of the c10 at the start of the passage. A fuller description of scrollable fields can be found in the **Vifred** section of the manual.

7.6.2 Date data

The absolute date in INGRES is comprehensive, as it includes day, month, year, and time according to the 24 hour clock. This means that the default size of the display format is -c25. If this is a little large when all you want is the date as eight characters, surely you can reduce the size of the field and make the format -c8? Sorry, but life is not that simple. The full format of a date display is Wed Jul 04 1990 15:35:40. Using -c8 would give you Wed Jul. So there must be some other way, and there is the date format. This may take some explaining, but it is not wasted effort, as the report generator and report writer programs use the same style of date templates.

A date template can be regarded as a mould which has a real date in absolute format put in, and the values of the absolute date modified in appearance coming out. The INGRES date template is made up of a string of special characters enclosed in quotes, determining which parts, and how the absolute date is displayed. These special characters are a representative date, the values of which are swapped for the date values you want to display. The representative date in absolute date format is Sun Feb 03 1901 04:05:06p. Weird, but there is logic there.

The representative date breaks down into the following parts.

Sunday represents the day of the week, and is the first day of the week.

1, 01, or 1901 represents year

2 or 02 represents month

3 or 03 represents day of the month

4 or 04 represents hour

5 or 05 represents minute

6 or 06 represents second

p or pm represents am or pm

This is intended to be easy to remember , as Sunday is the first day of the week, and all the other arguments 1,2,3, etc. are the year, month, day, etc. respectively. I don't expect to please all readers with the bald statement that Sunday is the first day of the week.

Format	Input Data	Report Output
d"2.3.1"	23- nov-1989	11.23.89
D"3.2.1"	6-jul-1989	6.7.89
d"03-02-89"	6-jul-1989	06.07.89
d"Feb, 01"	12-sep-1989	Sep, 89
d"February 3rd 1901"	15-may-1989	May 15th 1989
d"Feb"	25-dec-1991	Dec
d" 3 February I 01"	12-jan-1989	12 January 89
d" 3 February I 01"	5-may-1989	5 May 89

Figure 7.7 Date template examples

This is not the place for the quoting of scriptures and religious tracts from all over the world, as there would have to be many editions of this book and INGRES manuals to satisfy even the great religions of the world on this point. There is probably somewhere out in the world a group of people who believe Tuesday is the first day of the week. As far as this book is concerned, if I have got this wrong, don't write and tell me, as I won't reply. Back to the real task here, explaining the use and point of date templates.

It is probably far easier to use some examples to illustrate the use of templates, as you can see in Figure 7.7.

First of all you can see that before you put in a template it is necessary to tell INGRES that you are describing a date template. This is done by making the first character d, followed by double quotes and the template. The templates all use the representative date in some form or other. From the examples it is easy to see the effects; using Feb instead of February brings out the name of the month in a short three letter form.

One symbol in the templates that has not been mentioned is the vertical bar (I). This symbol causes all of the following output to be aligned, ignoring the length of the preceding value. This is used where different length month name would cause a column of dates, in a tablefield for example, to be displayed with the day of the month being displayed out of line. This action also holds true for different lengths of days of the week and any values which may have shorter lengths for different values. Look at the two bottom examples in Figure 7.7.

Any character not included in the special template characters will be displayed as they are, for example any spaces you put in the template will also appear in the final output. Don't forget, you can only use the numbers and names of the representative date to build a template, 1,2,3,4,5,6, remember.

Exercise 7.10

*Move to the **start_date** field on the layout form. Edit the display format of date to a date template which shows the date in "dd/mm/yy - hh - mm" format; check the example date templates in Figure 7.7.*

Edit the display formats for end date as well. Try out your edited fields by running your form by using QBF.

7.6.3 Integer data

The default display format for integer data is iN where i indicates integer, and N the number of digits to be displayed. This will normally default to the right size for the column width you have chosen. If you edit the format make sure it is large enough to hold the value to be displayed. For example if you have a column in a table of data type integer1 you can only enter values of -127 and +127. Trying to display data that is too large for the window would just cause INGRES to fill the field with asterisks. If you use a format of i3 trying to display 4453 would cause three asterisks to be displayed instead.

There is often a need to display the sign of a number to tell you if it is positive or negative. Just think how happy the banks would be if there were no overdrawn customers, because there were no minus numbers! To upset all the happy smiling bankers out there, make your display format wide enough to accommodate both the digits and the sign (+ or -). You can use numeric display templates, but after the previous section I will leave you that joy until the chapter on reports.

7.6.4 Numeric floating point and money data

Again our old friend the default display format helps here. A format of f6 will display six floating point digits. If you have a floating point number and you are only interested in the first two decimal places use f6.2, which displays the number rounded up to the second place of decimal, with five digits. A possible problem here is the use of a format that is not large enough for the number that you want to display. To save truncation and other embarrassments use the g symbol in place of the f. The g symbol tells INGRES that if there is enough space display the number as a true floating point, but if not display the number in scientific notation. If you are unsure about scientific notation, have a look in the manual.

Money data can be treated in the same way, but there are some interesting things that can be done with templates, but we will look at that in the chapter on reports.

7.7 Chapter Review

This chapter has taken the approach that once your screen looks good it is necessary to improve the functionality by including templates to make the data display in a more acceptable form. Another important area is the use of validation in a **Vifred** customized form. One of the important uses of **Vifred** is to include validation in the form definition. Using the form on its own by a QBF name will give a great deal of flexibility, but using a **Vifred** form from within ABF gives the added flexibility of a programming language.

7.8 Quick Reference

Edit Attributes from Edit Form Screen

- Move cursor to field for editing

- Select **Edit**

- Select **Attributes**

- Make changes

- Select **End** to finish editing

Comparisons

        fieldname   comparisonoperator constant

        fieldname comparisonoperator   otherfieldname

Referential Integrity

        fieldname in tablename.columnname

Edit Display formats

- Move cursor to field for editing

- Select **Edit**

- Select **DisplayFormat**

- Make changes

- Select **End** to finish editing

Chapter 8

Producing Reports

8.1 Reporting on Data

This is it, this is the part of INGRES that you can use to keep your job. Imagine, there is a panic on, the chairman wants some figures from the accounts database, but all the programmers are down with Flu. Who can save the day but Report Person. This super hero, can't you just see yourself, flies to the rescue, producing a draft report on screen and then dumping it to the printer with a flash of the fingers.

Still that is what it might seem like if you really are called on to produce a report quickly as it is possible to use defaults on views and tables bringing the report up almost instantly.

Reporting is the most visible part of the system and is usually the most open to criticism or praise. The reports that are produced on screen and paper are the main output of most systems. This chapter will take you through producing simple reports on tables to producing tailored reports with group totals, averages and all the goodies that make your heart sing.

This chapter will not be covering the INGRES Report Writer language. This language is generated by the menu driven tool, Report By Forms (RBF), but is sufficiently complex to fulfil many reporting needs. However the complexity and range of the report writer commands would make this chapter as large as the rest of the book.

8.2 Basic Reporting in INGRES

Before going to look at report production in detail it is important to understand a few basics.

The easiest method of producing a report is to say, in effect, "INGRES, give me a report on the customer table". This would currently produce a blank stare from your terminal, as computers generally can't talk. If however you gave a similar command to the reports subsystem, INGRES will respond by displaying, filing or sending to the printer the contents of the customers file, formatted and sorted, and looking more or less like a report. Of course you will need to make sure you type in the request, rather than say it, as we still haven't got a voice interface fixed.

RBF - Report Catalog

Name	Owner	Short Remark
default_report_operator	petem	rbf default report on operator table
equipment_in_stock	petem	Equipment in stock, sorted by equip_id
calls_logged	petem	calls_logged, daily report

Place cursor on row and select desired operation from menu

Create   Destroy   Edit   Rename   MoreInfo   AutoReport   Utilities   Go >

Figure 8.1 Report by forms menu frame

8.2.1 Reports catalog

As with most INGRES commands, it is possible to start RBF from the command line or INGRES Menu. To start from the command line use rbf dbname, but I will leave you to work out how to get into RBF from INGRES menu. Whichever way you choose to start RBF you will see a catalog of available objects and a menu to make your choices, an example of which you can see in Figure 8.1. It is also possible to run a report direct from the command line, via RBF, so after you have got to grips with this chapter a quick look at the manual should give you all the additional information you need.

Exercise 8.1

Start RBF from either the command line or INGRES menu. You should be viewing the RBF Report Catalog, looking like Figure 8.1. Select **MoreInfo** *and have a look at the menu that it offers. These are the normal INGRES options, so you can have a look at their effects and then return to the reports catalog. Carry on with the chapter now.*

8.2.2 Components of a report

A report has a number of components. Each report will have a title and date, columns of data, sometimes with column headings. Reports will have lines of data, distributed throughout the columns. These are called the detail lines, as they give the detailed body of the report. Finally there are page numbers at the bottom of each report page.

A little tip here, if you are planning some really large reports, beware, you can only have a maximum of 999 pages in a report. What a blow; there goes any chance of using RBF to prepare your personal expenses. Take a look at Figure 8.2 which shows a typical page from a report, and identifies the components.

8.2.3 AutoReport

One of the nicest parts of RBF is its ability to give you a report very quickly, as I have mentioned. If you select **AutoReport** from the report catalog, INGRES, still being polite, will ask you for the name of the table that you want a report on. INGRES then asks for a report format. What a demanding piece of software you may think. Finally, after what may seem like 20 questions, you are expected to press the **Return** key or enter a filename and press **Return**. After a slight delay INGRES produces the report. There is more about running reports later on in the chapter.

One of the real plus points about AutoReport, apart from simplicity and elegance, is the ability to start it from the Tables Catalog frame. All you have to do is place the cursor on the table that you want to report on, and select **Report**. From there on it behaves as though you had used AutoReport form the RBF catalogs frame.

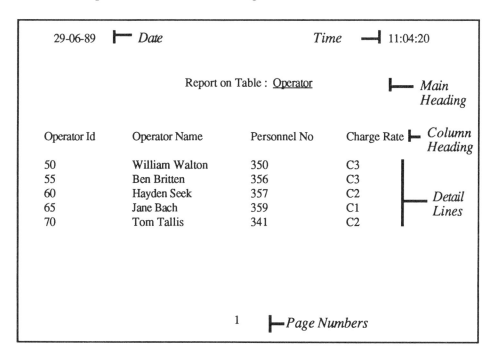

Figure 8.2 Component parts of a report

Sorry as I am to pour cold water onto your enthusiasm for this method of producing reports, there are, not surprisingly, some things that

AutoReport cannot provide. AutoReport will only produce all the data on a table, there are no facilities for data selection. Data is presented as it is stored in the database. There are no facilities for reformatting the data to be displayed, and also no facilities for accumulating or carrying out calculations on the data presented. Finally the report format is fixed and cannot be edited or modified. However don't be discouraged, as there are facilities for producing all these effects within RBF, and very simply too. For the moment though we will continue our walk through some of the common terms used in reporting.

29-06-89			11:04:20
	Report on Table: Operator		
Operator Id	Operator Name	Personnel No	Charge Rate
50	William Walton	350	C3
55	Ben Britten	356	C3
60	Hayden Seek	357	C2
65	Jane Bach	359	C1
70	Tom Tallis	341	C2

Figure 8.3 A column formatted report

8.3 Report Formats

INGRES RBF supports three report formats, without programming.

Other styles can be accommodated, but they still fall into the three basic formats of **block**, **wrap**, and **column** modes. What is the default format? All will be revealed in a moment. Before proceeding however, it is important to emphasize that these formats only affect the way that the data is presented, and not the data in the tables.

20-jun-90					13:30:29
		Report on Table: equipment			
Equip Id	Equip Desc		Stock Bin	No in stock	Reorder Level
	Price	Location	Unit Cost		
7780	Two Hole Punch		12	44	5
	2.30	W1	1.20		
7760	Mahogany Two Dr/Desk	10		2	1
	340.00	W1/F1	75.00		
7781	Leather Blotter Holder		12	4	1
	34.56	W1	25		
			1		

Figure 8.4 A wrap formatted report

8.3.1 Default format

INGRES once again demonstrates its intelligence here. If you select a default mode report INGRES will try to use **column** format, as detailed below. If however your data cannot fit into the columns across the screen or paper INGRES will switch your format to **block**. INGRES will estimate at 132 columns if a printer is specified or the width of your screen from the termcap file. For further information on termcap files ask your system manager or look in the INGRES Forms and Menus and Report Writer manual for your system.

8.3.2 Column format

In **column** format data is shown in columns across the screen or paper. If the data to be fitted into your screen or page is too wide then it is either trimmed and not displayed or it is wrapped around onto the next line. This depends entirely on the way in which your terminal or printer is set up. Figure 8.3 shows a column formatted report. You should be able to estimate the width of the report from the data that is being reported on. If you have three varchar(30) fields in your table then an 80 column screen will not take all that data in one line. If you are unsure, choose default format and see what decision INGRES makes, and take it from there.

8.3.3 Wrap format

Wrap formatted reports are similar to column formatted reports. As I said in the previous section INGRES will wrap data around the screen if there is not enough space on one line. Selecting wrap format will wrap data around the screen or printer, even if your screen or printer is not set up to autowrap. This is an alternative to **block** format for wide reports. Figure 8.4 shows a report in **wrap** format.

8.3.4 Block format

Block formatted reports show a line of data at a time, on the report, with the data identifier immediately to the left of the data. We can't really call the data identifier a column header, as we are not formatting the data to be in columns. The data identifier is normally the primary key column of the table. Figure 8.5 shows a block formatted report.

Exercise 8.2

To start this exercise you should be looking at the RBF catalogues frame for the exercise database that you have been using for all the other exercises.

*Select **AutoReport** and when asked for a table name enter **operator**. INGRES will then ask you for the format of the report. Select **default** format and press return to send the report to the screen. What format is the report in? Repeat this using the **default** format of the **customer** table. Is there a different format for this table?*

*Now select **AutoReport** specifying the **operator** table again, and this time tell INGRES that you want to see a **block** formatted report. After you have examined the output, try the **customer** table and select **column**, **wrap** and **block** formats in turn. Make sure that you have seen all three different formats and their effects. This will help you in future decisions about user formatted reports.*

21-aug-89   09:20:56

Report on Table: equipment

Equip id: 7780   Equip Desc: Two Hole Punch   Stock Bin: 12
No in Stock: 44   Reorder Level: 5   Price: 2.30
Location: W1   Unit Cost: 1.20

Equip id: 7760   Equip Desc: Mahog Two Draw   Stock Bin: 10
No in Stock: 2   Reorder Level: 1   Price: 340.00
Location: W1/F1   Unit Cost: 75.00

Equip id: 7781   Equip Desc: Leather Blotter Holder Stock Bin: 12
No in Stock: 4   Reorder Level: 1   Price: 34.56
Location: W1   Unit Cost: 25.00

                                  1

Figure 8.5 A block formatted report

8.4 Report by Forms

8.4.1 Using default reports

As I have already mentioned AutoReport gives you some features that are simple to use, but to get more flexibility from the reporting system it is important to edit and enhance the somewhat crude formatting produced by AutoReport. However there is still one use that you can make of the default reports. Saving a default format report as a user defined report makes it faster to produce. This is because the report formatting commands are held in the database; INGRES doesn't have to go to the trouble of calculating the formatting commands fresh every time.

8.4.2 Defining a report

After you have decided what you want your report to look like select the **create** option and then answer with a table name on which you are going to report. After that you are given a submenu asking for the format of the default report. Once you have replied with the format INGRES then shows you a frame giving the layout of the report. You can then take the decision to **edit, delete** or enhance the format before saving it. Take a look at Figure 8.6 which is a layout frame based on a **column** formatted report of the operator table. You will be using this later in the chapter for exercises.

Exercise 8.3

*From the RBF catalog frame select **create** and give **operator** as the table name that you are going to produce the report on. Make this a column based report and wait until INGRES displays the layout form. Don't take any other action for the moment as you will first need to learn what sort of action you can take.*

8.5 Changing Report Formats

Once you have got as far as producing a report layout you can decide whether you want the format you are presented with, or, as is more likely, you can decide to make some changes. Popular changes can be producing more meaningful headings and printing sub totals on each page. In this section you will learn how to **move** and **edit** layouts, as well as undoing the changes you have made.

There are three areas for editing in the layout frame: the title area, the column heading area and the detail area. These areas are clearly marked on the layout form and you move from object to object using the same key you would use to move around **Vifred** form layout frames. The **tab** key, as you may remember, is usually the one for this.

```
------------ Title ------------------------------------- Title -----------

                        Report on Table:  operator
--------- Column-Headings -------------------------- Column-Headings -------

Operator Id        Operator Name         Personnel No        Charge Rate


---------- Detail Lines------------------------------- Detail Lines---------

i_____        c_____        i_____             c_


--------- End-of-Detail ------------------------------End-of-Detail --------




Create   Delete   Edit   Move   Undo   Order   ReportOptions   Save   Help   End   Quit
```

Figure 8.6 Operator report layout

8.5.1 Editing trim and headings

This is simple. Move the cursor to the object that you want to edit and select, have a guess, **edit**. This will allow you to **edit** the object. The default method of editing is the overstrike, where every character you type in replaces an existing character. You can change this by selecting the **insert** key. If you are unsure of the correct key to make this change use **Help** and **Keys** for guidance. As you can only work with one line of trim at a time, you must move to another line before editing it.

When you have finished your edit press the **Return** key or the **Menu** key. Be careful about the return option, as it can destroy your edit from the cursor position to the end of the line. This depends how your system has been set up.

It is better, if you need to move objects, to use the **Move** option, rather than trying to use the delete or backspace key.

Exercise 8.4

*Move the cursor onto the title and select **edit**. You can only do this if you have left the screen on the report layout frame form after the last exercise. Change the title of the report to "Current Operators List". Move the cursor to each of the titles, and make any changes that you see fit. You may wish to change the abbreviations for the complete words, to make the report more readable.*

8.5.2 Moving objects

Like the **Vifred move** option, selecting move after placing the cursor on the object to be moved will bring up a submenu. Unless you have started this chapter after a long layoff, you should remember the menu options and their actions.

Left, Right and **Centre** moves the object the cursor is on to the leftmost, rightmost or centre position according to the margins of the report. The **Right** and **Bottom** margins of the report can be moved by placing the cursor on the margin and selecting **Move**. This will bring up a submenu which will allow you to **Move Expand** or **Place** the margins to change the shape of the report.

```
  ------------ Title ---------------------------------------- Title-----------

                      Report on Table:  operator
  --------- Column-Headings ----------------------------- Column-Headings -------

    Operator Id        Operator Name         Personnel No         Charge Rate


  ---------- Detail Lines------------------------------------ Detail Lines---------·

    i_____          c_____      i_____              c_


  ---------·End-of-Detail ------------------------------End-of-Detail --------



  Place     Left    Center    Right    Shift    Column    Help    End
```

Figure 8.7 Move submenu options

Have a look at Figure 8.7 and the submenu shown. Most of the options we are already familiar with, and some of these I have already written about, however there are a few options that are not familiar from other submenus. **Place** and **Shift** behave as the **Vifred** options, and put the moved object where the cursor has been placed, shifting other objects as needed.

A new option is the **column** option. This only appears after you have placed the cursor onto a column heading. Taking the column option tells RBF to move the column heading and the column data as a unit. If you don't choose **column** you will find that RBF treats the columns and their headings as separate units. Once you have chosen to move the column as a whole you can use any of the **Move** submenu options.

Exercise 8.5

*This is where you move the objects that you have edited. Make sure that you are on the RBF report layout frame and move the cursor to the **title**. Select **Move** and **Center** to get the title into the centre. Use the move and column options to exchange the positions of the operator id column and the personnel number column. You can have a try at exchanging the names of the columns only, if you wish, but be sure to change them back before using the form in anger.*

8.5.3 Creating objects

You may find yourself from time to time needing new objects on your report layout, and this is the shop you visit to get the new objects: just place three pounds of gold in a box and send to the address that the publishers will provide. An alternative method is to take the **create** option from the layout menu and check the new submenu. One of the things that I haven't told you to do yet is most important. You must place the cursor on the screen where you want the object to be created BEFORE selecting create.

Creating lines and trim is easy. Select those options and either a blank line is created or you can type in the text of a new piece of trim at the cursor position. A new heading line or a new column heading can be created by selecting the **heading** menu option. You must associate the heading with an existing heading by placing the cursor in the title or heading area. If you want to create a new column heading you place the cursor on the column in the detail area. This will cause the cursor to make a new line immediately above or below the exiting heading. If no heading already exists then the cursor is moved immediately to the headings section above the column needing the heading. Wow that was a mouthful, but a little practice may clear up any confusion. Now is the time to try Exercise 8.6.

Exercise 8.6

*From the RBF layout frame for the operator table, move the cursor to the title area near to the current title. Select **create** and create a new blank*

*line. Now create a new title. I would suggest a line saying "Author - "
followed by your own name. Move this line to the centre of the report.
Create some trim, for example some hyphens, to separate the two title
lines, and make sure that it is moved to an aesthetically pleasing position.*

*Finally this is your chance to create an additional heading for the
operator id column. Move the cursor to the detail area and place it on
the data definition for operator id. Select Create and Heading. Type in
"for Call checking". This should add the new title underneath the existing
one.*

8.5.4 Don't panic

This is where INGRES provides the comfort factor of being able to
Undo, or roll back the last edit. This will allow you to look at a report
definition and decide that the last move or create or delete did not really
enhance its beauty. INGRES will allow you to retreat to the comparative
sanity of your start point if you **Exit** without saving your report. The
Undo command will only **Undo** the last operation, retreating without
saving will **Undo** all of the last editing session. This of course assumes
that you have saved the form at least once before.

8.6 Data Display Formats

Once you have edited the headings and other finery you can move the
cursor down onto the detail area of the form and edit the data display
formats. This is very similar to the display format editing you have
already done in Chapters 6 and 7 on **Vifred**.

8.6.1 What you get for nothing

When you enter a report definition you are presented with a familiar
sight: for each column the format of the data is taken from the table
definition, and you will see the indicators for the column contents, **i** for
integer, **c** for character, etc. The number of underscores represent the
anticipated size of the data, so a **c** followed by 11 underscores tells you to
expect a 12 character display. If you need further details on default

formats, look at Figure 8.8. However if you are insatiable for new sensations you can edit those display formats and produce startling results.

Data Type	Default Display Format
Character	Character (c)
integer1	f6
integer2	f6
integer4	f13
float4	n10.3
float8	n10.3
date	c25
money	$--------------.nn

Figure 8.8 Default data display formats

8.6.2 Numeric templates

In **Vifred** I didn't spend too much time on numeric templates, as it is in the reports that money and numbers are most frequently represented as formatted. Numbers, represented in the databases by integer and floating point, etc. are just numbers but they are not very meaningful. Presenting 25467344 without any sort of punctuation makes the number almost meaningless. Including punctuation, for example 25,467,344 makes the number easier to assimilate. So, how do we achieve this result? With the ubiquitous template, as you have probably guessed.

A template, as you may remember is a kind of mould for your data, you press your data into the mould, like clay, and the mould changes the way your data looks, without changing the data itself. Following the analogy, the mould must be constructed of special materials, for repeated use. The kind of materials we use are detailed below, but they must be enclosed in double quotes. If you are still confused, look at Figure 8.9, which shows some templates, the numbers used for the example and the way in which the number would be printed.

Some of the characters that we use for templates are replaceable characters, that is, if there is a number in the position the character is replaced by the number or the template character is printed. Others are printed if there are still numbers to be printed, either at the end of the number or the beginning.

n	Print the digit, if there is one or print zero if not.
z	Same as "n" but print a blank if there is no number.
$	If there is a digit left in the number print the digit, but if not, print a money sign to the left of the first digit printed. Sounds confusing I know but there are some examples later on to help you understand.
-(minus)	Print a digit if there is one there, but print a leading minus sign if the number is negative, or a blank if the number is positive.
+	Almost the same as the minus, but in this case the leading character is a plus if the number is positive, and a minus if the number is negative.
,(comma)	This is where you get the punctuation for large numbers. If there is a digit then print the comma in this position. For example with a number 2345 and a template "nnn,nnn,nnn" you would get 2,345 as the result.
.(decimal point)	Print the decimal point in this position.
*	If no digits are left print an asterisk. This would be useful for printing cheques.
space	Print a blank space in this character position. You can also

do this by using the back slash (\).

CR   This will print the characters **CR** after a positive number, and blanks after a negative number. You can print these in either upper or lower case, or a mixture, depending on how you specify them. So now you know how the banks print your statements; you probably see these after your pay cheque has been cleared.

DR   These characters are probably more familiar. They will print after negative numbers with a blank after positive numbers.

\c   This is sneaky. If you precede any character by a backslash, that character is printed properly instead of being regarded a part of the template. If, for example, you wanted to print a "z" in a number for punctuation you could use "nnn\znn" and a number like 2345 for 23z45 as the result.

If you look at Figure 8.9 you can see the results of various templates and their results. The caret (^) symbol in Figure 8.9 indicates a blank, or space.

8.6.3 Date and time templates

As you can remember from Chapter 7 date and time formats were discussed in depth. So if you need to refresh your memory, turn back a few pages, and read with fascination and awe, as the mystery is solved.

8.6.4 Changing data display formats

Now that I have told you what you can use templates for and what they can do for you, I suppose the next thing is to tell you how to enter your chosen templates into your report. All you need to do is to move the cursor onto the column that you are going to use the template with, and select **Edit**. Choose the **DisplayFormat** option and type in your template, making sure that the template is enclosed in double quotes.

Format	Example Data	Report Output
"*zzzzzzzzz*"	123	^^^^^^^123
"*zzzzzzzzzz*.nn"	0	^^^^^^^^^00
"++++++++++"	3456	^^^^^+3456
"$$$,$$$,$$$.nn"	23456.666	^^^$23,456.67
"$$$,$$$,$$$.nnCr"	+23456.666	^^+$23,456.67

Figure 8.9 Examples of templates

After you have finished keying your template, press the **Menu** key to finish. Simplicity itself, but now is the time to try one out in Exercise 8.7. Although Exercise 8.7 only deals with a trivial sort of template, it is just a practice; there will be other template editing for different style reports.

Exercise 8.7

You should make your way to the report layout frame for the operator table that you have been editing and move the cursor to the operator id column. Edit the display format of the operator id column to make all the leading zeros appear. A little hint: look at the examples if you are not sure. End your edit of the display format and return to the report layout frame.

8.7 Saving Report Definitions

8.7.1 Saving reports

After all the painstaking work on editing your report it would be a pity if it were left in the limbo that all good work goes to, so it needs saving. Saving your report is the same as saving all the other INGRES objects that you have created; the details of the report definitions are held in the database catalogues, ready for recall when the report is run. To save the report in the database catalogues choose the **Save** option and you will be presented with the Save Report Frame similar to the example in Figure 8.10. The **Forget** option will let you return to the previous frame without saving your report. From the Save Report frame you can choose **End** or **Quit** which are standard options, and if you have made some changes that haven't been saved INGRES will ask you if you are sure, and if you are sure that you want to finish your edit without saving, then carry on.

You should treat the short and long remarks in the same way as you did for **Vifred**, using them to maintain records of changes and the purpose that the report will be used for.

If you are editing a report that you have already saved, INGRES will only show you an edit submenu, which contains the **Save**, **EditInfo**, and **Forget** options. Save and Forget work as I have already mentioned but the new option EditInfo will allow you to make changes to the short and long remarks for the report, before you save the report.

8.7.2 Saving as Report Writer code

One of the classy options in RBF is to archive the report definitions as report writer code, giving a head start to producing a more complex and sophisticated report. Report Writer is a part of INGRES that uses a programming type language to define report layouts and the data that you can retrieve. It is important for producing very sophisticated reports, giving you many features that RBF cannot. However it is a great deal more complex and would take up probably another book to cover it in any depth. You may want to try using Report Writer later in your INGRES experience so it is useful to know how to produce some code from your menu driven definitions.

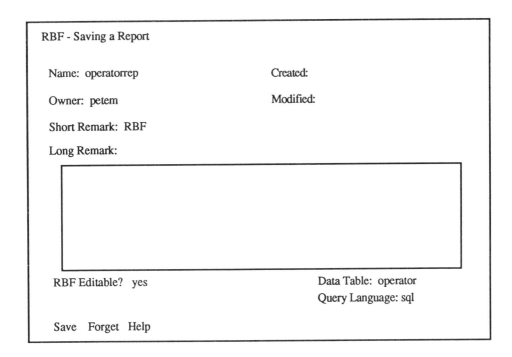

Figure 8.10 Save reports frame

Once you have saved a report selecting **End** will take you back to the Reports catalog frame. Place the cursor over the name of the report that you want to archive and choose the **Utilities** option. From the submenu that is displayed selecting the **Archive** option will prompt you for a file name. Put in a file name, like "myreport" and INGRES will add the extension ".rw" to it. This will tell report writer that the contents of the file are code. To follow this you can read the INGRES Forma and Menus and Report Writer manual, which will explain the delights of the **sreport** command, and give details of how to edit your code, and run it with the **report** command.

Exercise 8.8

Unless you have read ahead and already done so, now is the time to save your report. Select **Save** *from the menu, and follow the instructions on the Report Save frame; you can see an example in Figure 8.10.*

If you have saved your frame successfully you will see the Reports catalog and, what a coincidence, you are just in the right position to archive your report as Report Writer code. Move to the menu line, if **Archive** *is not in the display window, and select* **Archive**. *Re-read section 8.7.2 if you are not sure about naming the report file. If you want to view the report writer code you will need to exit back to the operating system and use a command like* **type** *"filename".*

8.8 Running Reports

As we have already looked at producing an Auto Report this section will only deal with producing a report from report definitions. There are two ways of producing a report: you can use RBF and the **Go** option, or you can run the report direct from the command line. There is a third way, using an application frame, but we will cover that in the next chapter.

8.8.1 Printing on a screen

To run a report from within RBF life is simple, all you need to do is make sure that you are looking at the RBF catalog frame, place the cursor on the saved report definition and press **Go**. Finishing by pressing return instead of putting in a file name will send your report to the screen. Once on the screen the report will structurally appear either like Figures 8.3, 8.4, or 8.5.

Running a report from the operating system is easy if you use the syntax below, in fact if you don't you won't get anywhere.

```
report dbname reportname.
```

If you replace `dbname` with your database name and `reportname` with the name of the report that you want to see, and press return, the report will be formatted and printed to the screen.

An important part of running a report on a screen can be seen if you look at the menu line on the bottom of Figures 8.3, 8.4, 8.5. This menu line has three selections.

The first menu option, **C**, continues scrolling the remainder of the report on your screen without stopping, unless you use the terminals "brakes". Pressing the **control** key and the **s** key together will stop the screen scrolling or pressing the **control** key and the **q** key will start the scrolling after it has been stopped by **control s**. This neat little trick is not specific to INGRES, and is a feature of a number of operating systems.

The second menu option, **S**, stops the report display and returns you to the RBF catalog frame, the application frame or the operating system, depending from where you started.

The **Return** option will display the report a screen at a time. If you have any problems with this it may be a good idea to check your terminal identity and setup with your system manager, when he has got back from the bar.

8.8.2 Saving the result in a file

Saving a report in a file is easy from the RBF catalog frame. When you select **Go** to run the report INGRES will ask you for the name of a file. In the previous section I suggested that you use the **return** key to accept the default display, but if you enter a file name the report is sent to that file in a continuous stream. You can then read the report without having to re-run the report. However the report on file will only reflect the state of data when the report was run, not when you read it. This file could then be merged in with other documents and used in a wordprocessing file to build up complex documents, or sent to a printer, as we look at later in the book.

Sending the report to a file when you run reports from the operating system is even easier: all you need to do is add the **f** flag and immediately follow it with a file name. Don't forget flags always prefixed with a - (minus) sign. For example:

```
report exercises customer -fcustrep
```

will send a report, saved under the name customer in the exercises database to a file called custrep.

Where do these files go when they are written? Into the part of the system that you are sitting in at the moment, usually your home directory.

Exercise 8.9

If you are still looking at the reports catalog, try placing the cursor on the name of your saved report and run that report. Now is a good time to try running your report from the command line, saving the output in a file or putting it to the screen.

8.8.3 Sending to a printer

Once you have sent your report to a file it is then possible to use the operating system commands to send it to a printer. However there is another option: there is a key word PRINTER. Using that instead of the file name used in the previous section INGRES will put your report to the system printer. However if you want to use a special printer the system administrator can give you help.

8.9 Selecting Data in RBF

In default format and AutoReport reports the only data you get is the data in the table that you have named, and you get it all, whether you want it or not. To make the reports more effective it is sometimes necessary to select data according to some criteria. Typical selections could be all the orders that are between two dates, or only employees who work for a particular department. Adding selection to the ability to produce subtotals and grand totals gives you the flexibility to apply these reports to real business problems.

8.9.1 Break columns

A break in a column occurs where the values in a column change, for example when a department name changes in an employee file. This can be used to control the printing of subtotals, for the department, for example. Lines and other objects can be printed to highlight the break between one group of data and the next group of data. One important point, each column to be regarded as a break column must also be a sort column. Sort columns are the columns on which the report data has been sorted on. Taking the employee table mentioned earlier, if the report is printed in alphabetic order of department then the break column is department, and it is also the sort column. The section on modifying sort order will give you further information on sorting.

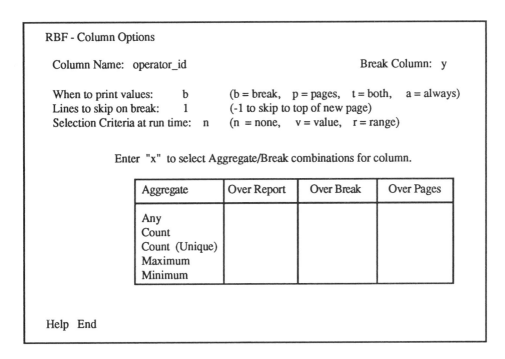

Figure 8.11 Column options frame

Looking at Figure 8.11 you can see where to specify when to skip lines, and print aggregates, counts, etc. over the whole report or breaks or pages. More importantly you need to put a "y" in the **Break** column in the **Order Column** frame, as you will find in a later section. This is how a "y" appears in the **Break Column** field of the **Column** Options Frame.

8.9.2 Column options

Figure 8.11 is an example of a Column Options frame. RBF only displays all of these options if you are working on a sort column. You can use this frame in RBF to suppress the printing of repeating values in a break column to make the break more obvious. This can be done when you specify "b", for break in the "when to print values" field.

"Lines to skip" is the field where you put the number of lines in between blocks of data. This makes breaks more obvious.

8.9.3 Aggregates and counts

The aggregate column has different entries in according to the data types of the column. If you think about it, it is pretty difficult to add up the values in an address or name column; all you can do is **Count** the number of entries. **Maximum** and **Minimum** will print their respective values. **Count** and **Count unique** will print the number of entries in a group of data or the number of unique entries. The **Any** option will print a number 1 if any value exists or a 0 if no value exists. **Average** and **Sum** will do their duty for all the numbers in the list.

The other columns on the form tell RBF when to print the values that have been selected. You must put a lower case **x** in the appropriate column, upper case **X** or another value will not work. If you specify a value **Over Report** then the value will be printed once, underneath the detail column specified, at the end of the report. **Over page** prints at the end of each page, before the next page, and **Over Breaks** at the end of a break in a break column. This is where **Nulls** come in useful, as the use of a default entry in a column, rather than a null may produce bad counts or sums.

Exercise 8.10

*In this exercise we are going to use **Column order** and **Count** to produce a report on the **equipment** table.*

*Create a report layout on the equipment table and change the default sort order. Make the break column **bin_number** and **Count** the number of items in each bin.*

*When you have completed your edit, **Save** and **Run** the report. You will notice that the figures for the count of bin items is under the bin_number column, and the only way of identifying the figure is the word **count** in the left-hand column.*

RBF - Order Columns

Scroll through the column names. Select the sorting sequence (0 - 127), sorting direction ("a" or "d") and whether to break (" y" or "n") for each column.

Column Name	Sequence	Direction	Break?
eqip_id	1	a	y
equip_desc	0		
stock_bin	0		
no_in_stock	0		
reorder_level	0		
price	0		
location	0		
unit_cost	0		

ColumnOptions   Top   Botton   Help   End

Figure 8.12 RBF order columns frame

8.9.4 Run time data selection

To specify data to be selected at run time you have three options. The first is "n" for none; when the report is run it will not stop to ask you for any more information, just churn on with the entire table as input.

The second option is **v** for value. This will make RBF stop when you run the report and ask you what value do you want to print the report on. For example if you entered "29.03.90" in a date field it wouldn't work, as you need to enter a recognizable date, like 29-mar-90. But, forgetting the error, the absolute value of the date would tell RBF only to select and print rows having that date. All the other rows would not be printed as they don't match the selection criteria. One awkward point here, you must put in the whole date, you can't use wildcards to select all the dates in March, or all the values greater than 3345. For that you need the range option.

Entering an **r** in the field will prompt you, when the report is being run, for two values, no wildcards again. This time however INGRES will print all the values between the ranges specified. When you use this option, on a column like Unit Cost on the equipment table INGRES will ask, always polite, for a Start Unit Cost and an End Unit Cost. When you have put in two values INGRES will ask you to wait as it is selecting the data and formatting it before producing the report.

8.9.5 Modifying sort orders

The sort order determines the order in which data is presented in a report. There is a default. If you don't do anything INGRES makes the assumption that you want the first column in the table as the break column. Default sorting order is **ascending**, in date, numbers, or alphabet, depending on the data type. From there you are on your own, having to make changes to definitions to change preconceived notions.

Selecting **Order** from the RBF Layout frame will bring you to the Order Columns frame, as in Figure 8.12. This brings up an entry in the table field for each column in the report detail line. For each of these column names you have the option of specifying which of the columns is the first in the sorting order by an entry in sequence column. As you can see from Figure 8.12 the default order is a 1 in the first column, equip_id with all the others having a 0 entry. If 2 is entered in the stock_bin column then the report is output in **ascending** order of equip_id and **ascending** order of stock_bin when there are duplicate equip_id numbers.

To change the direction of sorting is also very easy: just enter an **a** for the **ascending** order or a **d** for **descending** order. Finally the only change that you may need to consider is specifying any break columns. To do this enter a lower case **y** in the break column of the Order Columns frame.

Exercise 8.11

For this exercise edit the saved report from Exercise 8.10. When you have the report layout form on the screen, edit the column options for equipment_id and choose runtime data selection. All you need to do then is put in a value for equipment_id to get a list of all the items in bin_number order. Save and Run your report. Does this make any difference when the report starts? If it doesn't then you must have done something wrong, go back, check and try again.

8.10 Selecting Data Using SQL

Although RBF will only allow the production of reports on single tables, no joindefs; there are ways around this. There are two ways that can be used, the first method is to create a new table, the second is to create a view.

The easiest way to create a new table and populate it is to use an SQL command. This command **create table as** will build and populate a new table, on which you can carry out your new found skills of report definition. For example

```
create table newtab as select * from oldtable
     where age = 30
```

produces a new table called newtab which contains identical columns to the table oldtable. All the data from oldtable is retrieved and placed in newtab providing the values in the age column are equal to 30. This would produce a table where all the age entries are the same. The SQL statements that I have mentioned can be keyed in and executed using an INGRES terminal monitor. Details of how to do this can be found in the INGRES SQL manual. This command can restructure the data or tables and demonstrates some of the power of the SQL language.

8.10.1 Creating views

Another method of using SQL, this time to get data from joined tables, is a **view**. A **view** is a logical table that can be made up of one or many physical tables. This logical table is not held as an object in the database, except in description form. Views can include selection qualifications as suggested in the SQL code example above. Views are able to provide the report with data from more than one table. If you feel that you will need to use views in your applications read about **select** clauses and **views** in the SQL manuals.

8.11 Chapter Review

In this chapter you have covered the most visible part of most systems, the reports that are produced. The use of the AutoReport, and defined reports have been investigated. Editing and customizing report layouts and saving reports have been covered in some depth. The concepts of SQL and multiple table reports were introduced.

8.12 Quick Reference

Starting RBF

```
rbf databasename
```

Using AutoReport from the Reports catalog

- Select **AutoReport**

- Select format of the report, **block, wrap, column**

- Enter a file name and press return to write report to file

- Press return only to send report to screen

Using Default Reports

- Select **Create**

- Enter a table name

- Select the format required

Edit trim and headings

- Move the cursor to the trim to be edited

- Select **Edit**

- Make changes

- Select **End**

- Select **Undo** to reverse your change

Edit DisplayFormats

- Move to trim

- Select **Edit**

- Choose **DisplayFormat**

- Select **End** to complete the edit

Chapter 9

Tying it all Together

9.1 Applications by Forms

As you are now completely aware this book is built around a number of menu driven tools. At least you should be aware of this if you have followed the rest of the book. If you are just browsing in the book store, you are probably going to be confused.

You can skip this chapter all together if you wish. It is not essential if you are going to use the tools on their own, from **Ingmenu** or the command line. This chapter will allow you, however, to replace Ingmenu with your own menu, more specific to your needs.

Although INGRES is based on menus and the concept of visual programming, user friendly applications need some sort of glue to tie objects together without having to use QBFName catalogs and Reports catalogs. Any of the objects for accessing and manipulating your database can be easily linked together in an application that can be started from the command line. A menu system can move you from customer maintenance to call entries, and back. Now you can see why we spent so long on designing the hierarchical menus for our exercise database. The part of INGRES that provides the glue is a menu based system itself, called Application By Forms or ABF. This chapter will unfold the mystery of creating applications from a variety of 4GL code, frames, forms and other objects.

9.1.1 Forms or frames?

A form is a vital part of INGRES, and you have been using them all along. As a form in INGRES is merely an electronic version of a paper form, why make all the fuss? Simply, an INGRES form is a screen into which you will place data, or display data.

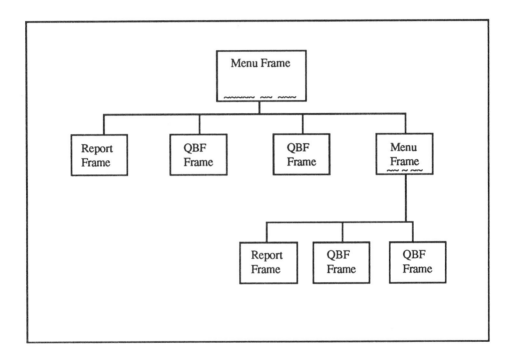

Figure 9.1 ABF structure overview for an application

A frame however describes not only the form, but the attendant functionality. In QBF a frame has data entry fields, and the functionality is provided by INGRES, automatically. To produce more complex and sophisticated functionality INGRES allows you to enter commands in a computer language called INGRES/4GL. This language, a little of which you will learn in this chapter, is sufficiently complex to be able to create major league applications, but is still simple to learn and very productive.

As each statement in the language is evaluated it generates the equivalent of many instructions in a "lower level" language like "C". So, forms are data entry/display screens, and once they have some underlying functionality, with menu choices, operations, validations and other glitzy items, they become frames. Therefore the **Vifred** Form layout screen is a frame, with functionality to produce a form. Once you have saved the form you have created, you can only access data by turning it into a frame. Associating the form with QBF in a QBFName or adding some 4GL code produces that transformation. The reason for labouring this point, apart from padding the book out, is to emphasize the fact that frames, backed by QBF, RBF or 4GL are the basic building blocks of an application.

```
ABF  -  Applications Catalog


   | Name            | Owner | Short Remark           |
   | call_details    | petem | Call Logging           |
   | operator_maint  | petem | Maintain Operator Files|
   | customer_maint  | petem | Maintain Customer Files|




             Place cursor on row and select desired operation from menu.

  Create  DEstroy  Edit  Rename  MoreInfo  Go  Utilities  Find  Top  Bottom
```

Figure 9.2 ABF catalog frame

9.1.2 What does your application give you?

An application can give you almost anything from delight to ulcers, but primarily an application is a collection of functions that fulfil your needs as a user. If you are developing the application for your own use you might find communications problems between users and developers a thing of the past, although you may end up talking to yourself. The application will normally start with a menu that is started from the command line with a one line command. All you need to do to gain access to the various parts of the application is to enter menu choices and away you go. Simple is it not?

9.2 Starting ABF

ABF is a menu driven system and as such has the inevitable start point for all menu driven tools, the catalog frame. When you start ABF you are presented with the ABF catalog frame, from which you can create new applications and edit existing ones. So before we start fooling around with an application it is probably best to learn to start ABF and create an application to play with.

9.2.1 From the INGRES menu system

To start ABF from the INGRES/Menu system, you should be able to guess at the selection of **Application**. From there INGRES takes your hand on the difficult path to the ABF catalog. An example of an ABF catalog frame is shown in Figure 9.2.

9.2.2 From the command line

To call ABF from the catalog first take some chalk and draw a large pentacle, stand in the middle and chant "Om" for seven hours, after a three day fast. A better method is to type in the words `abf database-name application-name`, and let INGRES again conduct you gently to the ABF catalog.

9.2.3 Creating an application

Once you have an ABF catalog frame it is then possible to create an application. This is easily accomplished by selecting **create** from the catalog frame menu. INGRES then takes you to the, guess what? Create an Application frame, that's what. This frame has a few fields for you to complete before you can work on an application. Take a look at Figure 9.3 while you are reading this section.

When you are first shown the application creation frame it has **unspecified** in the name field. If you really want to name your application unspecified, then INGRES will object and tell you so. However you may wish for a more understandable name to your application so move the cursor, if it is not on the name field, and enter your application name.

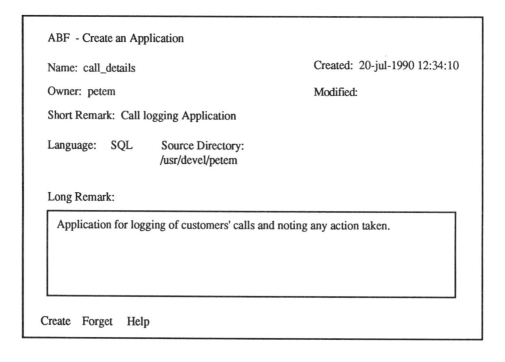

Figure 9.3 Create an application frame

From now on I am going to assume that you can carry out simple tasks like moving the cursor without explanation because INGRES frames all behave in a similar fashion.

This is the place to change the source code directory if you wish. You may find that your organization has some form of standard directory structure or location for source code. You may wish to talk to your system manager about this. Source code is defined in the glossary, if you are not sure.

Long remarks and short remarks can be included here, giving you the opportunity to show your documentation skills. Use wisely and these can save if not your life, at least your job, or a significant time in understanding a complex application.

Once you are happy with the name and other features of the create an application form, selecting **create** from the menu line will create your application and take you to the Edit an Application frame with a number of fields, like the default start frame name, and the query language name already filled in. Figure 9.4 is an example of the Edit an Application frame which will be used in the next section.

Exercise 9.1

*From either the command line or INGRES/Menu start ABF on your exercise database. Select **Create** from the catalogs frame and put in the name for your application, and a short remark about the application. If you think there is more information about the application than can be expressed in a short remark, remember that it is useful for other people or your own memory to have full information on any object.*

*After you have completed the form **create** the application and when you find yourself back at the Edit an Application frame try **MoreInfo**.*

9.3 Frames and Definitions

ABF applications are made up of frames and procedures. Procedures can be written in 4GL or a programming language like "C", but the frames have screen forms prepared by **Vifred** and functionality provided by INGRES. INGRES can provide you with functionality in two easy to swallow capsules, 4GL or "Canned Frames".

```
ABF - Edit an Application

    Name:  call_logging                    Default Start:  topmenu
                                           Query Language:  SQL
```

Frame/Procedure Name	Type	Short Remark

```
        Place cursor on row and select desired operation from menu.

Create   Destroy   Edit   Rename   MoreInfo   Go   Utilities   Find   Top   Bottom
```

Figure 9.4 Edit an application frame

A canned frame is a frame with the functionality already provided by INGRES. Forms can be prepared for some of the canned frames that require data entry, like RBF needing run time selection criteria, but mainly canned frames use default forms. A canned frame expects the developer to enter some style of response, table names or object names for example and uses those to integrate the objects into an application.

The other type of frame is the user defined frame. This is a frame with **Vifred** generated forms and underlying 4GL code. A little later you will learn how to use some 4GL just to manage the complete application from a series of menus.

Creating any frame follows the same basic path. First you select **create** from the edit frame, then select whether a **frame** or a **procedure** is required. After that select the type of frame and away you go.

This is where the book gets overloaded as there are three frames to describe. The first frame, the edit an application frame, is shown in

Figure 9.4. After selecting the create menu item a part of the screen is over written by another small frame, creating a window. This is the create a frame or procedure pop-up. An example is shown in Figure 9.5. If you were wondering about pop-up frames in the chapters about **Vifred**, this is how a pop-up frame works, giving a window with its own menu and functionality. The processing of the main frame is suspended whilst the pop-up frame is displayed, control being passed back to the mainframe or another pop-up depending on the 4GL code in the pop-up.

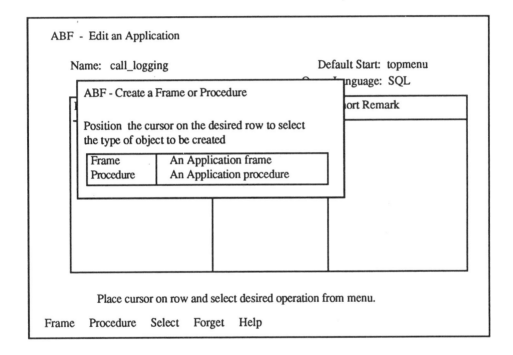

Figure 9.5 Create a frame or procedure pop-up frame

When presented with the create a frame or procedure pop-up frame you will see a menu appear on the bottom of the main frame. Most of the selections from this menu are old friends. However **select** will let you choose the part of the table field that the cursor is placed on. Choosing **Frame** or **Procedure** menu items selects the respective object type and takes you through to the next pop-up frame. For this book we will only be looking at frames, so your next pop-up frame is the create a frame pop-up, where you can choose what type of frame you are going to work on. Figure 9.6 is an example.

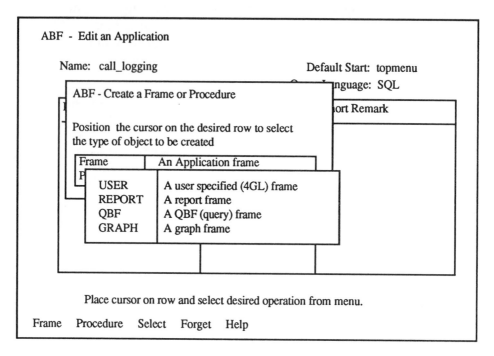

Figure 9.6 Create a frame pop-up

The next pop-up is overlaid on the base frame and the frame/procedure pop-up. This gives you an opportunity to select the type of frame. The user defined frame is one we will deal with later. For the moment we will look at the canned frames to use. There are three types of canned frames, the **REPORT** frame, the **QBF** frame and the **GRAPH** frame. As we haven't covered graphs in the past we will still leave them to one side now.

9.3.1 User defined frames

A user defined frame is covered in more detail in the section about creating menus. All you need to know for the moment is that user defined frames consist of 4GL code and a **Vifred** created form.

9.3.2 QBF frames

A QBF frame is simply a method of calling a QBF user interface like a QBF name or a table default from within ABF. Once you have called a QBF frame it behaves the same as if you had started it from the command line. Then to create a QBF frame select **Create** from the Edit an Application frame, and when you have specified **Frame** select the usage type **QBF**.

A pop-up frame for creating a QBF frame is then shown, giving you the option to enter a name for the QBF frame or forget the whole thing and go back to the previous frame. Forget is an option that you will see a lot of during ABF sessions, and it always means the same: go back to the previous frame, and undo anything you have just done.

After entering your name for the QBF frame and selecting create the screen changes, the music starts, and you are into the twilight zone. Getting exciting now, eh? Well it really is fairly exciting as you are about to see your first application frame built. The screen that you see is the Edit a QBF Frame Definition frame. What a simple title, redolent of meaning. If you look at Figure 9.7 you will see a sample already completed. As we go through the next part keep that frame in mind as I will be referring to it.

There are a number of menu options, some of which are again INGRES standards, but some are interesting, also they are common to other frame definition frames.

The **NewEdit** option selects a different object for editing. The **Edit** option edits the query or the JoinDef for the query. A new option is **FormEdit** which allows the creation of a form for the table or joindef you have specified in the Query Object. You should be familiar with the use of **Vifred**, so I won't tell you more about customizing a form.

If you look at Figure 9.7 there is a field with a default form name in. If you haven't got a form already you can put a name here and use **FormEdit**. Don't worry about a message telling you that INGRES can't find a form, as you may not have created one yet. When you create a form and save it you don't have to save it as a QBF name as ABF will do that for you.

ABF - Edit a QBF Frame Definition

               Frame Name: call_in_j

        Query Object Name: call_in_j
                     (Table or JoinDef)

        Query Object Type: JoinDef
             Form Name: call_in_j
      Commnad Line Flags:

   Short Remark: This is a QBF Frame drawn on the call_in_j joindef

   NewEdit   Go   Edit   FormEdit   MoreInfo   Print   Help   End

---

Figure 9.7 Edit a QBF frame definition

INGRES is very helpful to users: it assumes, with some reason, a number of defaults. When you look at the edit frame you can see a frame name that you have put in the previous frame. The query object type is assumed to be a table, and the name of the table and the form name are assumed to be the same as the frame name. You can change these, if you wish, by moving the cursor and editing the appropriate field. If the query object you name is a JoinDef then you will need to change the name in the query object type field from table to JoinDef. It is always possible to enter a short remark here.

One of the really great performance aids in ABF is the ability to check that the canned frames are correctly specified and do their job properly. All that is needed is to select **Go** and let ABF start the frame for checking. Selecting Go will start QBF, in this case, on the named query object and let you use all the functions of QBF.

A nice touch is the ability to specify and use command line flags in ABF. For example if you type **-mretrieve** in the command line flags field QBF is started in retrieve mode. If you can't remember all the command line flags refer to the chapters on QBF and the INGRES manuals.

Once happy and delighted in your frame all you have to do is exit back to the Edit an Application frame and this part of your application development is completed.

Exercise 9.2

*Using the section above as a guideline create a frame that will run QBF on the **operator** table. This frame should be familiar from your original work on the exercises in the chapter on Simple Data Manipulation. As this frame is going to be part of the operator file maintenance functions in your specification you should give it an appropriate name; **addoperator** is the sort of name.*

*As you are going to use the form for adding new operators the form should have a **Vifred** tailored form with suitable trim. More importantly you will need to edit the form defaults to name the operator table as the query target and the command line flag is mode **append** only.*

*Now you are familiar, more or less, with creating QBF frames you should practise a little. Try defining a frame for the Joindef you created in the exercises at the end of the chapter on complex data manipulations. If you used that joindef as the basis for editing exercises in the chapters on **Vifred**, so much the better as you don't have to recreate the customized form.*

9.3.3 Report frames

Report frames are handled in a very similar fashion to QBF frames, but there are a few additional points. The frames are created in the same way, except the usage is REPORT, but there are a few differences in the Edit a

Report Frame definition frame, as you can see from Figure 9.8.

Once you have the Edit a Report Frame definition frame on screen you need to enter the name of the report and then look at all the other goodies that are laid out for you.

```
ABF - Edit a REPORT Frame Definition


            Frame Name:  customerrep
            Report Name:

         Report Source File:
            Report Form:
            Output File:
         Command Line Flags:


   Short Remark:  This is a report on the customer file










   NewEdit   Go   Edit   Copmile   FormEdit   MoreInfo   Print   Help   End
```

Figure 9.8 Edit a REPORT frame definition

If you have specified a source code file, one that you have prepared with an editor, in report writer commands, INGRES will start an editor if you select **Edit**. If you leave the source code field empty, pressing **Edit** will call up RBF for you. If you use RBF the **Compile** option is not active, as you don't need to compile code that is not there.

An important option here is the output file field which can contain the name of a file into which the report placed. Also the report can be sent to the terminal or printer by specifying special file names, terminal or printer respectively.

Forms are used for matching symbolic parameters to fields on a form. This is covered in report writer and ABF manuals. Command line flags are used here in the same way that they are used in QBF frame definitions.

Exercise 9.3

Check the name of an RBF report that you created in the last chapter and use that name in defining a report frame. Don't forget that you have the same option here as in QBF and can check the report you have defined by selecting **Go**. *After you are happy with your definition of the report frame, and checked it with* **Go**, *press End and return to the Application Definition frame.*

```
ABF - Edit a User Frame Definition


       Frame Name:  topmenu

     Form Name:  topmenu
     Source File :  topmenu.osq
     Return Type:  string
         Nullable:  no


   Short Remark: This is the topmenu frame for the application








  NewEdit    Go    Edit    Compile    FormEdit    MoreInfo    Print    Help    End
```

Figure 9.9 Edit a USER frame definition

9.4 Creating Menus

Now we are in the position of having some frames that are going to use as part of our application, but how do we use them? Is it always entering ABF and running the frames by Go, or is there another way?

As you have already guessed, the way that we have to tie all these different elements together is to write a menu. This is so fundamental to creating an application you may have wondered why I didn't start the chapter with this, but it is easier to create a user frame as a menu after you have used some of the other frame definition frames.

Before you create a menu you will need to go by a familiar route, by creating a frame and defining it as a user style frame. Once you have done that you are presented with an Edit a User Frame Definition frame, an example of which is shown in Figure 9.9.

You will see that the name that you gave the frame when you created it is in the Frame name field, well what a surprise. Some of the menu items are familiar, but we will examine the new options one at a time. Since a frame is a form plus functionality the first thing to do is to create a form for the menu.

9.4.1 Vifred in ABF

Selecting **FormEdit** from the user frame editing frame will take you to **Vifred** using the name that is in the form name field as the default form name. If the form doesn't exist in the **Vifred** form catalogs, you will get a message telling you that the form doesn't exist. Pressing Return at the "No form found in the forms catalog" will move you to the forms catalog letting you create a form. The sort of form you create for a menu is made up of trim, and put into a blank form, so you would select **BlankForm** as the option to create a form.

A menu usually tells the user what options there are and ties those options to an action, like pressing the F1 key or making a selection on a menu line. The menu form only needs the explanatory trim. I will show you how to put in the menu line later. Look at Figure 9.10, an example of a menu created from a blank form.

A little tip is always handy, and this is one of the best. If you are editing or creating forms for use with ABF, do the editing from within

ABF. **Vifred** forms that are created and any edits not done within ABF do not show up in the application, as ABF saves the forms in a different way from **Vifred**.

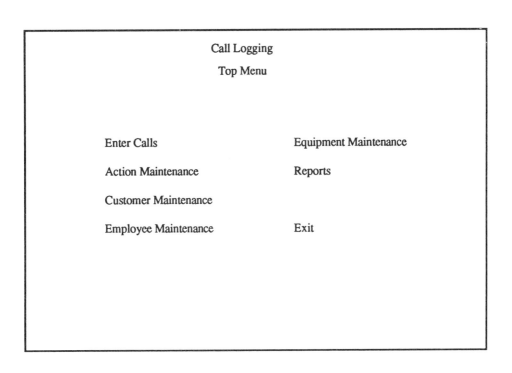

Call Logging

Top Menu

Enter Calls   Equipment Maintenance

Action Maintenance   Reports

Customer Maintenance

Employee Maintenance   Exit

Figure 9.10 Sample menu form created in **Vifred**

Exercise 9.4

*Create a user defined frame called topframe. Once you are shown the Edit a User Frame Definition Frame select **FormEdit** to edit a new form. Press Return when **Vifred** tells you that the form topframe is not in the forms catalog, and select **Create** and **BlankForm** in **Vifred**.*

You are going to create a form to control the frames that you have already defined. So create some trim in the same style as Figure 9.10, but make sure that you include menu items for at least one of the reports that you created and at least one of the QBF frames. The other item you must not forget is an Exit or End menu item. For the moment if you are not sure use the following menu items, and follow them through into the other exercises, or use the layout in Appendix G.

```
Menu items: QBF Frame 1, Report Frame 1, Exit.
```

Once you have created your form, don't forget to save it, and then exit back to the User edit frame. Await the next instructions, Mr Phelps.

9.4.2 Calling other frames

Once a form has been created it is time to create the code that will provide the routing for your application. This code is written in a new language that you will only scratch the surface of in this book, INGRES 4GL. To start your creation, attach the electrodes to the neck bolts and fire up the generator. The other alternative is to select **Edit** and follow ABF into a system editor. This is one of the more difficult parts of the book, as there are a number of system editors available, including some word processors. If you are working on a VMS machine you will probably use EDT, which is quite easy to use. UNIX based systems always have the vi editor, but most will have some other, more user friendly editor. However, vi is not difficult, and once you really get into using it you will be pleased by the flexibility and power, but it does take time. If you are using a PC the default text editor is edlin, and may the Lord have mercy on your soul. Edlin is not my favourite editor, but there may be someone out there who likes it.

Once you are into the editor display you have a number of options, but I would take the one that starts with strong drink. The first thing to look at is the overall construction of 4GL code. This code is different from most programming languages because it doesn't matter what in order you put the operations - you can select any one in any order. 4GL code is grouped into operations, for example, using English statements. We can define operations, before coding, in the following way.

```
Add a record operation
     Get data
     Check data is correct
     Add a record to the database
```

```
      End the add a record operation
Delete a record operation
      Get the data from the database
      Do you really want to delete this record
      If you want to delete the record, delet it
      If you don't want to delete it end the delete a
      record operation
```

These operations are independent of each other. It should not matter in which order you choose the operations. For this reason INGRES/4GL used to be known as an Operation Specification language.

This may make for some confusion and unlearning. The general structure of the language is simple. Each operation consists of a block of code preceded by an activation.

```
activation  = begin
          other 4GL statements;
     end
```

You will notice that there are few punctuation marks, but what is there is important. An activation is the start of an operation, and there are a number of different types. You make a choice or commit an action, or even by doing nothing you can initiate an operation, We are going to look more closely at menu activations, that is starting an operation by making a menu choice. You should consider, however, that there are field, key, timeout and initialization activations. Your manual or training courses can probably tell you more, if you are interested.

The menu activation defines the name of the menu selection for display on the user's screen menu line. so if you start a menu activation with "Reports" then the menu line will show the word "Reports" on, and normally a function key will be assigned for you to press to start the report's block of code.

The other job of the menu activation is to specify a series of 4GL statements to be executed each time the operation is selected. If we look at an example, perhaps it will become clearer.

```
'Reports' = begin
          callframe reportfrm;
     end
```

This statement will place a menu item with an associated function key on the menu line of the report frame that you have defined. The statement in between the begin and end starts a frame called reportfrm, which you may already have created. You can put many more statements between the begin or end. If you have defined a number of frames, QBF frames, user defined frames or reports frames then you can call or start them by using callframe followed by the name of the frame you are going to call. One important point is the semi colon. If you miss that you won't get the frame to compile, as it is the semi colon that tells INGRES that you have finished your statement. If you look at Figure 9.11 you will see a block of code, the form that the code is associated with and a look at the final result. It may help you to visualize how things hang together.

I have not mentioned comments yet, and now seems like a good time. Comments, which are not regarded as part of the code, start with a /* and end with a */. Anything written between these symbols will not be regarded as 4GL. Look at Figure 9.11 to see an example of comments in action. The intention behind comments is to allow descriptive sentences to be read as part of the code, but ignored by the system.

```
"Enter Calls" = begin
                        /*call callin frame */
                        callframe  call_in;
                end


"Action Maint" = begin
                        /*call action frame */
                        callframe  action;
                end


"Exit"        = begin
                        /* Exit from frame */
                        exit;
                end
```

Figure 9.11 Code and callframe statements

Exercise 9.5

Now is your chance to revisit your programming youth, and after he has given you tea and cakes start writing a controlling menu for the top frame of your application. If you are having problems, check the code section in Appendix G before continuing.

*Select **edit** and enter the text needed to control your menu choice. Make the first option the same as the first menu item. Don't forget that the frames you are going to call in this demonstration application are the frames that you created earlier. You must remember to include all the parts of the menu activation, and especially the **begin** and **end**. Once you have completed your edit leave the screen as it is; the next exercise will be to add extra statements.*

9.4.3 Exiting from frames

When the time comes to finish with your application you must make arrangements to exit quietly. Although it is possible to break the application using control keys, or by terminating the process that is running, these methods will leave temporary files and permanent files in some turmoil. Only use this method in extremis. INGRES has two statements for ending the execution of a frame, **exit** and **return**. **Return** will stop the execution of the frame whenever it is reached, and return you to the next frame above in the hierarchy or the operating system if you are at the top of the hierarchy. If you have had a lapse in memory about menu hierarchy and the way in which ABF causes you to cascade frames, take another look at Figure 9.1.

Exit is the statement that ends your application taking you back to the operating system. This is the best way to exit from the application, but you can use a mix of **return** and **exit** to control the use of your frames. As you can see from the code sample in Figure 9.11 **exit** is used as a single word, followed by a semi colon, and between the **begin** and **end** keywords.

9.4.4 Compiling frames

Once you have finished putting your code into the editor **exit** from the editor, saving the code, there is no need to supply a name for the code as INGRES will supply that. INGRES will now display the User Defined frame definition frame, and from here you can take the **Compile** option. This option takes the code and form and processes them through some software called a compiler, which takes all the items together and converts them into a form that can be run by the computer. If there are problems with your code or the frame you have defined there is a checklist to look through in section 9.7, but most of the problems are easy to sort out. INGRES will give you an error message. A common problem is to spell a keyword wrong or use the wrong command. Another is to miss off the semi colon. Exercise 9.6 will give you some practice with compiling and debugging your code.

Exercise 9.6

This exercise is a follow up from the last one, and you should still be looking at the system editor screen into which you typed your 4GL code menu activations.

As the text of this chapter has emphasized, you must leave an exit to prevent you having to break the running application with control C. Type in the exit menu activation, and if you are not sure that you have entered the correct code take a look at the code sample in Appendix G.

*When you are sure that you have created a **Vifred** form containing menu text, and some code, created in the system editor, **exit** to the frame definition frame and compile the frame by selecting the compile menu item.*

This is where the fun begins, as you may have made some mistake in creating or editing your frame and you need to find and correct all the errors. There are a number of things you can check, so go through the debugging checklist at the end of this chapter.

9.5 How to Start Your Applications

There are two ways to start applications: one is to start from within ABF, using the **Go** option; the other is a little longer in execution, as you create an executable image. The go option from the ABF catalog frame is used for testing frames without going to the lengths of creating an image.

9.5.1 What is an "image"?

An image is a special file in a format and with contents that are compatible with your operating system. The image is a snapshot of the application, and you cannot edit an image, but this is the form in which your application should finally be. As you are then independent of ABF, the application behaves like any other executable program. To create an image, select the **Image** option and you will see the build application image frame. This will give you the chance to go back, by taking the end option.

The default name is the name of the application, but that can be changed if you wish. Building an image is time consuming, up to five times longer than using the Go option.

9.5.2 Testing your application

To test your application, even if it is not complete, use the **Go** option from the edit an application frame. This runs the application using dynamic linking and doesn't take so much time. This is the best way to test your application, as you can start the application from any frame you want to name in the hierarchy. If an application is started from a frame part way down the hierarchy it is not possible to move back up the hierarchy, beyond your start point.

When INGRES is ready to go, it will ask you for the name of the frame to call. Give the name of the frame you want to test from or the top frame in the application. Then all you have to do is respond to your application to see it run.

9.5.3 Undefined frames

Don't worry about incomplete applications, as INGRES will see your callframe command calling a frame that doesn't exist. It then makes the assumption that you will be defining it in the future and just displays an undefined frame. Enter a new frame name or press return to go back to the calling frame, to carry on.

One little problem with ABF is its reluctance to let you test out the application having a frame that won't compile. You either have to have entirely undefined frames, or incomplete frames that will compile, or of course the immaculate and truly wonderful frames that you have completed as a result of reading this book. So although the application is not complete it is still enough to be tested.

Exercise 9.7

This is the final exercise in the book. Run your application by using the **Go** *option from the application definition frame. If you have finally completed your application then you can* **image** *the application and try running it from the command line. Check out the section on running images in the ABF/4GL manual for your system.*

9.6 Chapter Review

In this chapter you have probably covered more ground in a shorter time than you expected. You will have gone from creating canned frames to creating a user defined frame. You will have used one of the many types of activations, the menu activation, and entered some 4GL code. After all this you will have a complete application that you can run from the operating system command line, but more importantly some firm building blocks onto which you can stack other INGRES skills to develop more and more sophisticated applications. It only remains for me to thank you for coming on this journey and I look forward to our next meeting.

9.7 Quick Reference

Debugging Checklist

This is where you find that you have used a reserved word in your code, like "desc" for descending. That and typographical errors are the most popular type of errors.

Have you created your screen form from a blank form?

Have you created some 4GL code?

Have you spelled **callframe** correctly?

Has each of your menu activations got a **begin** and **end**?

Have you given your menu item a name that is a reserved word but not enclosed it in quotes? If you are not sure about reserved words look in Appendix F. Avoid using reserved words.

Is your callframe statement terminated by a semi colon?

There may be other reasons for a compilation failing, so if you are really sure that you have done everything correctly, and your code looks like the sample in Appendix G, there may be nothing for it but to scream to your system administrator for help, or to go back, destroying the menu frame you have created and re-create it to see if that makes any difference. There is not much more that I can do if you still have problems, so you may well have to admit defeat and read the manual.

Epilogue

Hey, what's happening?

Now you have come to the end of this book, what can you do next? The first thing that springs to mind is relax and figure out how to apply your new skills. After a little thought I am sure that you can think of some application that is crying out for treatment. Once you have exhausted the skills gained from this introduction to INGRES you may wish to expand your knowledge and there are a number of routes you can take.

If you are looking to write professional applications the best route is a training course. These courses give hands on sessions and sound advice on developing applications and using INGRES in the most efficient way.

An alternative method is to use the manuals and ask your collegues for assistance. This is the slower method, and usually you will miss some vital background information. On balance the best aproach is to take a training course.

As new features are developed for INGRES rest assured that I will be looking to produce other user guides.

Finally, remember what you should have learned throughout this book. If you are not sure about something, try it out. You can't do much damage and you may discover something new in INGRES. Above all;

Have fun trying!

Peter Matthews

Appendix A

Exercise Database

Overview

The exercise database makes the assumption that any organization which deals with the public will receive telephone calls about orders, information and, occasionally, complaints. These calls if recorded on paper may sporadically be lost or mislaid. A computerized system for handling incoming calls and responses could provide the solution to lost call records, and provide sophisticated management information.

Call tracking systems are implemented by a large number of organizations who have a customer interface. For example, INGRES Corporation, the authors of the INGRES products, use call tracking for customer support and sales calls.

The design of the exercise database, its tables, forms, and reports are not intended as a complete example of a call tracking system, rather as building blocks to a more advanced system. However there are some additional columns in the equipment table that would need to be included if stock control and order processing were to be included in the future.

Functional Description.

The system is intended for on-line data entry of calls, logged in database files. The operator first enters their name at the start of the data entry session, and then as calls come in an operator asks the caller questions and fills in a screen form.

Some questions have to be answered to maintain the integrity of the data. These are mandatory fields on the form. Some of the questions are either/or type questions. The following fields are mandatory in the customer call entry section:

> Customer Number or Customer Name
> Equipment Identifier or "General" Classification
> Problem Description

Input of the Customer Name/Number will allow the extraction of customer details from the Customer File. Equipment identifier or general classification is checked on entry for a valid customer identifier and allows a link to be maintained between the call detail file and the equipment detail file. The problem description contains any details of problems or requests orders are noted and the details can be printed as a report. An order processing system could be added later if necessary. After problem entry further action can be logged as taken, or deferred, with the action file being updated as needed.

The action id is the operator id of the employee who is expected to take the action. The operator id is the identity of an employee who is taking the call, not necessarily the same identity as the employee taking action. During the day staff can display reports on the following data.

> Specific or all Customers.
> Specific or all Calls grouped by
> > Equipment
> > Operator
> > Customer
> > Action identifiers
> Specific or all Operators
> Specific or all items of Equipment
> Actions by call or action id.

Actions can be entered by entering the action form and adding new actions to the call. The call id is a mandatory field. This frame will allow the modification of the actions, but not the call details.

Customer, equipment, and employee details files are maintained by individual forms, which access the tables and allow the insertion, modification, and deletion of these details.

Forms and Menus

The following lists are the menus and the forms resulting from an analysis of the problem outline. These form the basis of all the main functions in the system.

Main Menu Selections

Enter Calls:	takes the user into the calls data entry screen. This screen is entered in append mode.
Action Maintenance:	takes the user to the action maintenance menu.
Customer Maintenance:	takes the user to the customer maintenance menu.
Employee Maintenance:	takes the user to the employee maintenance menu.
Equipment Maintenance:	takes the user to the equipment maintenance menu.
Reports:	takes the user to the reports menu, containing all the management information reports.
Exit:	Exits the application.

Action Maintenance Selections

Enter Actions:	allows the user to log new actions for specified calls.
Modify Actions:	allows the user to modify actions that are already logged.
List Actions:	allows the user to list actions by call id or all the actions for a single call.
Return:	returns the user back to the main menu.

Customer Maintenance Selections

Enter New Customer: allows the entry of new customer details.

Display Customer: displays customer details by all customers or specific customers.

Modify/Delete Details: gives a form that allows the modification or deletion of customer details.

Return: Return to main menu.

Employee Maintenance Selections

Enter New Employee: allows the entry of new employee details.

Display Employee: displays employee details by all employees or specific employees.

Modify/Delete Details: gives a form that allows the modification or deletion of employee details.

Return: Return to main menu.

Equipment Maintenance Selections.

Enter New Equipment: allows the entry of new equipment details.

Display Equipment: displays equipment details by all equipment ids or specific equipment id.

Modify/Delete Details: gives a form that allows the modification or deletion of equipment details.

Return: Return to main menu.

Reports Menu Selections

Customer:	Report on one or a range of customers.
All Customers:	Report on all customers on file.
Employee:	Report on one or a range of employees.
All Employees:	Report on all employees on file.
Equipment:	Report on one or a range of equipments.
All Equipment:	Report on all equipments on file.
Action:	Report on one or a range of actions.
All Actions:	Report on all actions on file.
Calls/Cust:	Report on all calls per customer.
Calls/Op:	Report on all calls per operator.
Calls/Act:	Report on all calls actioned by a specific action id.
Calls/Equip:	Report on all calls per equipment id.
Return:	Return to main menu.

Tables

The following tables can be entered via the tables utility:

Table Name customer

custno	integer
custname	varchar(20)
custcont	varchar(20)

custaddr1	varchar(20)
custaddr2	varchar(20)
custaddr3	varchar(20)
start_date	date
billing	char(2)

Table Name call

call_id	integer
custno	integer
operat_id	integer
start_tm	date
end_tm	date

Table Name call_details

call_id	integer
equip_id	integer
descrip	varchar(100)

Table Name operator

operat_id	integer
op_name	varchar(30)
pers_no	varchar(30)
charge_rt	char(2)

Table Name equipment

equip_id	integer
equip_desc	varchar(30)
stk_bin	smallint
no_in_stk	smallint
re_order	integer1
price	money
location	varchar(30)
unit_cost	money

Table Name action

call_id	integer
eq_id	integer
action_id	integer
act_desc	varchar(50)

Appendix B

SQL Scripts

These scripts are to be used in the INGRES SQL terminal monitor, called by the queries/SQL option from Ingmenu, or directly from the command line by using

```
isql <dbname>
```

from the command line. For further information, check the manual.

```
create table customer(
                custno          integer,
                custname        varchar(20),
                custcont        varchar(20),
                custaddr1       varchar(20),
                custaddr2       varchar(20),
                custaddr3       varchar(20),
                startdate       date,
                billing         char(2)
                );
create table call(
                call_id         integer,
                custno          integer,
                operat_id       integer,
                start_tm        date,
                end_tm          date,
                );
```

```
create table call_details(
                    call_id          integer,
                    equip_id         integer,
                    descrip          varchar(100)
                    );
create table operator(
                    operat_id        integer,
                    op_name          varchar(30),
                    pers_no          varchar(30),
                    charge_rt        char(2)
                    );
create table equipment(
                    equip_id         integer,
                    equip_desc       varchar(30),
                    stk_bin          smallint,
                    no_in_stk        smallint,
                    re_order         integer1,
                    price            money,
                    location         varchar(30),
                    unit_cost        money
                    );

create table action    (
                    call_id          integer,
                    eq_id            integer,
                    action_id        integer,
                    act_desc         varchar(50)
                    );
```

Once these create table commands have been entered into the INGRES
SQL terminal monitor (started by the command at the beginning of the
appendix), selecting **Go** will cause the statements to be executed. If the
statement fails, select **End** to return to the editing frame and make
changes. When you have completed your work selecting **End** will leave
the terminal monitor and commit your statements to be commited to the
database.

Appendix C

Test Data

These are the test data for some of the tables in the example database, Not all the test data is included, as data that results from JoinDefs can be created "on the fly".

Customer Table

Custno	Custname	Custcont	Custaddr1	Custaddr2	Custaddr3	Billing Code
271	Rex Head Motors	Charles Wells	854 Desborough Road	High Wycombe	Bucks	B1
273	The Model Shop	Martin Model	24 Packhorse Road	Gerrards Cross	Bucks	B1
472	Tomlin and Jones	Jack Jones	48 Castle Street	High Wycombe	Bucks	B3
475	Harlow Monroe Ltd	James Harlow	Pond View House	Bourne End	Herts	B3
46	Williams and Son	Sanjit Singh	Lower Gornal Way	Milton Keynes	Beds	B1
59	Wong Importers	Sam Wong	Lotus House	Aylesbury	Bucks	B2

Equipment Table

Equip_id	Eguip_desc	Stock Bin	No in Stock	Reorder Level	Price	Location	Unit Cos
7780	Two Hole Punch	12	44	5	2.3(	W1	1.2(
7760	Mahog. 2 drawer file	10	2	1	340.0(	W1/F1	75.0(
7781	Leather Blotter Holder	12	4	1	34.5(	W1	25.0(
7782	Desk Pen Holder	12	8	5	1.8£	W1	1.0(
7784	Metre Ruler	12	7	5	0.9£	W1	0.5(
7761	Executive Chair	9	2	1	241.0(	W1/F1	135.0(
7771	Ream 80g Pager	21	250	100	12.0(	W2	9.0(
7774	Ream 120g Paper	22	100	50	15.0(	W2	12.0(

Operator Table

Operator Id	Op_name	Personnel No	Charge Rate
50	William Walton	350	C3
55	Ben Britten	356	C3
60	Hayden Seek	357	C2
65	Jane Bach	359	C1
70	Tom Tallis	341	C2

Appendix D

Naming Conventions

INGRES objects can be named according to the following conventions, and they can have any names, except for any reserved words listed in Appendix F.

1. No more than 24 characters are allowed in a name

2. The first character of a name must be alphabetic (a-z), or the underscore character

3. After the first character other characters are 0 to 9, hash, @ and $.

4. Names are case insensitive. If you call a table Smith&Sons it will be converted by INGRES to smith&sons.

The final point to make in naming conventions is obvious, but needs saying again and again. MAKE IT MEAN SOMETHING! Meaningless names hinder any user, and waste time.

Appendix E

Data Types

c(*n*)   A fixed length string of up to 2000 printable ASCII characters, with non-printable characters converted to blanks.

char(*n*) A fixed length string of upto 2000 ASCII characters, including any non-printable characters.

varchar(*n*)   Variable length ASCII character string, up to 2000 characters.

text(*n*)   A variable length string of up to 2000 ASCII characters.

float4   4 byte floating point; for numbers including decimal fractions, from -1.0e+38 to _1.0e+38 with 7 digit precision

float8   8 byte floating point; for numbers including decimal fractions, from -1.0e+38 to -1.0e+38 with 16 digit precision.

integer1 1 byte integer; for whole numbers ranging from -128 to +127.

integer2   1 byte integer; for whole numbers ranging from -32,768 to +32,767.

integer4 4 byte integer; for whole numbers ranging from -2,147,483,648 to +2,147,483,647.

money 8 byte monetary data; from -$99999999999999.99 to +$99999999999999.99.

+$99999999999999.99.

date   12 bytes; ranging from 1/1/1582 to 31/dec/2382 for absolute dates
and -800 years to +800 years for time intervals.

Appendix F

Reserved Words

abort
all
alter
and
any
as
asc
at
avg
begin
between
by
byref
call
callframe
callproc
check
clear
clearrow
close
commit
copy
count
create
create integrity
create link

create view
current cursor
delete
deleterow
desc
describe
direct connect
direct disconnect
direct execute
distinct
do
drop
drop integrity
drop link
drop permit
drop view
else
elseif
end
endif
end loop
endwhile
execute
exists
exit
field

for
from
grant
group
having
help forms
helpfile
if
immediate
in
index
initialize
inittable
insert
insertrow
into
is
like
max
message
min
mode
modify
next
noecho
not

null	scroll
of	select
on	set
open	set_forms
or	sleep
order	some
prepare	sum
printscreen	system
privileges	sql
procedure	table
prompt	then
public	to
qualification	union
redisplay	unique
register	unloadtable
relocate	until
remove	update
repeat	using
repeated	validate
resume	validrow
return	values
revoke	where
rollback	while
save	with
savepoint	work
screen	

Appendix G

Answers to Chapter 9 Exercises

These are suggested answers for exercises in Chapter 9.

Exercise 9.4 Screen Layout

```
                          Exercise 9.4



             1. Run Report



             2. Run QBF Frame - addoperator



             3. Exit from Application



```

Don't forget the menu operations will also appear on the bottom of the form, placed there by INGRES/4GL code.

Exercise 9.5 and 9.6 Code

```
'Run Report' =   begin
                 callframe reportfrm;
                 /*
                 **    This applies if you have defined
                 **    a report frame in Exercise 9.3
                 **    and called it reportfrm.
                 **    Otherwise substitute your name
                 */
          end
'Run QBF' =      begin
                 callframe addoperator;
                 /*
                 **    If you have defined a QBF frame
                 **    in Exercise 9.2 and called it
                 **    addoperator use this statement
                 **    Otherwise replace addoperator
                 **    with the QBF frame name that you
                 **    used in Exercise 9.2
                 */
          end
'Exit' =         begin
                 exit;
                 /*
                 **    Bye, bye, finished now
                 */
          end
```

Glossary

A

ABF(Application By Forms)

> A menu driven application generation system. It is designed to build INGRES applications. From ABF it is possible to call all the INGRES subsystems including as well as a text editor.

abstract data type

> A data type that is not native to the system. An example of this is the **date** data type, which is a coded data type that is implemented by a data structure. Each data type, although there are currently only two, is also supported by functions, like the date interval. The other abstract data type is the money data type. User defined data types are also available.

attribute

> In **Vifred** an attribute is a characteristic, such as inverse video or query only, that affects the display and behaviour of a field. This is also used as another name for a table column.

B

back end

> This term should be replaced by the term database server system. This is the part of INGRES that interacts with the data and

communicates with the front end, or user interface, such as an application of QBF.

break column

This term refers to a column for which a special action must be taken when data values change. For example if the nominated column is the department column of an employee file it is possible to use a change in the department value to accumulate the number of employees in the department.

C

catalog

In database management terms a catalog is the name given to a special table which contains details of all the other tables and objects in the database. This special table is created and maintained by INGRES.

catalog frame

A special frame that contains details from the system catalogs of objects for manipulation, for example the **Vifred** catalog frame shows the names of all the forms saved within the database.

column

A vertical section of data in a table or table field that represents one piece of information. All the data in a column is of the same type, i.e all the data in an age column must be of type age.

D

data manager

This is the process that is responsible for the interface between the data and the user, see back end.

data window

The area on a screen form that displays or accepts data.

database

This is where it's at, as they say. A database in INGRES terms is a collection of tables, including the system tables, or catalogs that contain details about the other tables in the database that contain data, or the forms' details or reports' details.

dataset

A set of records that are retrieved by a query, for example a "Go" option in QBF. If you put a wildcard data selection or select Go without specifying any data QBF will retrieve a number of rows; those rows are the data set of the query.

default

This is something that is provided automatically. For example when you start QBF on a table with no other input, QBF uses a default form, which depends on the table details for its contents. A default value in data validation terms is an automatic value that is displayed, like today's date, but which can be accepted, for convenience, or rejected.

E

executable image

An executable image is a snapshot of an application. It cannot be edited, although the objects that are used to build an image can be edited. A new image can be created at any time. An image is an object code program that will work on runtime INGRES and does not necessarily need a development licence.

F

field

An area of a form used for data entry and display. This is made up of a title, a data window and data attributes. Data fields are normally edited or created by the user within a **Vifred** session. The other usage of the term field is as a synonym for column.

Field is used in non relational terminology to describe the smallest unit of data that has meaning in describing information. Used as a fractional part of a record.

form

The computerized equivalent of a paper form. Users can enter, store and retrieve data using a form.

frame

The pairing of a form and some functionality. In some cases functionality is provided automatically by INGRES, as in QBF or RBF. Functionality can also be provided by 4GL statements in an application.

front end

The user interface to the data manager. This can be an INGRES tool like QBF or it can be an application. It is sometimes called a client.

H

heap

The default storage structure for INGRES tables. This defines a table that has no indexes, no keys and no ordering.

I

index

See secondary index.

INGRES/MENU

The tools that allow access to INGRES's other front end or user interface tools.

J

JoinDef

A grouping of tables that have been logically joined together into one object for data retrieval purposes.

K

key

The part of a row that uniquely identifies that row. As each row needs to be unique INGRES adds a tuple id to enforce that uniqueness.

L

lock

A lock in a database is a mechanism that ensures that no other user can change the data that you are reviewing or amending until you have finished with it.

M

menu key

The key that moves the cursor from a form onto a menu line. This key also switches the hidden part of a menu line into view, should the menu line be wider than the screen.

man-year

A unit of estimating, roughly, the amount of work one person can do in one year. A five-man-year project could be completed in one year if five men were working on it.

O

object
Any database entity, a table, a form, frame, application, joindef, QBFname, etc.

P

page
The smallest storage element of INGRES data, 2048 bytes, with 2008 bytes available for user data, the rest is INGRES information.

Q

QBF(Query By Forms)
An INGRES tool that allows the user to execute queries or define specifications for joined files. Data entry or retrieval is effected by some standard functions based on default table structures, JoinDefs or QBFnames.

QBF name
A linking of a form to a table or a JoinDef. Normally a form that has been customized or edited using **Vifred**.

query
A statement that adds, deletes, updates or retrieves data from a database object.

query target
An object used in QBF. Query targets include tables, joindefs and QBF names.

R

RBF(Report By Forms)
An INGRES menu based editor for producing customized reports.

record
A set of data in a table, all of the data related and identified by a unique key. For example, in a personnel system an employee's name and address are related to each other and the other data items in an employees record by being related to the key, employee number.

relation
A table of data that is related by being part of a set, ie. an employee table contains data that is related by being part of the employee information. This could also be described as a flat, two-dimensional file. The basis of a relational database.

report
A listing of data from the database displayed in an easy to understand manner.

row
A set of related data in a table. See record.

S

schema
A map of the overall logical structure of the database.

secondary index
A table composed of a key and a pointer to the records of the base table. This is used to speed up access.

simple field
A field containing a single piece of data. Only one piece of data can be displayed at a time. See table field.

sort
> A term used for the rearranging of data in a specified order.

source code
> Programming language that cannot be directly processed by the computer hardware. Source code needs to be read by software called a compiler used to produce object code that can be used directly by a computers hardware

SQL (Structured Query Language)
> A language used to define, manipulate and protect data. Originally developed by IBM. SQL has now become the standard relational database query language.

storage structure
> A way of arranging the pages in a database table. INGRES has four major storage types. heap, hash, ISAM and Btree.

system catalog
> See catalog.

T

table
> A collection of data suitable for quick reference, each item being uniquely identified either by a key. Relative position in the table is not important in a relational database, as the key is the unique identifier.

table field
> A field displaying several pieces of data at the same time. One or more rows can be displayed in this way.

TABLES
> A forms based tool accessible from INGRES/Menu for creating, examining and deleting tables. In Chapter 3 you will also learn to modify tables.

title

> A character string on a form used to identify a field or trim to identify or explain a function.

trim

> A character string used to inform or enhance the use of a form.

tuple

> A group or related fields. See row or record.

V

validation check

> In **Vifred** a test to ensure that data entered in a field matches pre specified criteria.

view

> A logical definition of data taken from one or more tables linked together. A view can only be created by using a query language like SQL.

Vifred (Visual Forms Editor)

> The INGRES menu based editor for customizing forms.

Index

233